THE ULTIMATE DIMENSION

THE ULTIMATE DIMENSION

by

Juan Arias

Translated by

Paul Barrett, O.F.M. Cap.

ABBEY PRESS
St. Meinrad, Indiana 47577
1977

This is a translation of *L'Ultima Dimensione*, published by Citta-della Editrice, Assisi, Italy.

Nihil Obstat:
    Fr. Cuthbert McCann, O.F.M. Cap.
    Censor theol. deput.

Imprimi Potest:
    Fr. Anthony Boran, O.F.M. Cap.
    Min. Prov. Hib.

Library of Congress Cataloging in Publication Data
Arias, Juan.
  The Ultimate dimension.
  Translation of L'Ultima dimensione.
  1. Meditations. I. Title.
BX2182.2.A7413   242   76-43072
ISBN 0-87029-128-9

Contents

Contents

Preface

Modern man is beginning to get tired of useless objects and increasingly feels an urgent need for the plain, unvarnished truth and simple, genuine things.

But how is he to rid himself of the former, and where is he to find the latter?

He is beginning to feel surfeited and even overwhelmed by the machines, the political parties and the culture that hitherto he has had to accept.

We men of today are hungry for bread that is bread, for a little clean air and for even a few men who are uncontaminated, innocent, or at least just. However, we shall have to work hard to find them.

We have become too accustomed to looking for hopes and for gods outside ourselves, to handing over to mercenaries the management of our affairs in peace and in war, and, in the name of a system of values set up by a handful of leaders, to accepting too many chains, too many illusions, too many fears, and too many attacks on our consciences.

And this has wreaked havoc, sometimes almost fatal havoc, in the last dimension of our lives, the best part of ourselves, that part which allows us to savor life and live peacefully on our earth.

Our personal creativity and even our freedom of conscience have been stifled, and we have been made the victims of a vast scheme of manipulation aimed at controlling not only our actions but even our thoughts.

Like our first parents in the Garden of Eden after the Fall, we have come to realize that we stand naked in the new paradise that has been built, not in the name of creativity, but for profit. We, too, have become ashamed of ourselves and cannot look each other in the eye without blushing.

We feel unfaithful to ourselves and we regret the enormous plastic structure that we have built around us. We are filled with rage at seeing that we have allowed ourselves to be shaped by others and that we are not true sons of freedom.

We have put a price tag on everything and have even been tempted to offer ourselves for sale in the great market place of lies in order to auction off our very last dimension—our hope of beginning again, of rebaptizing the last words of existence, of speaking a new language in which we could use living words and not a glib sales patter; a dimension in which love cannot be confused with oppression, or freedom with order, or peace with immobility, or work with slavery, or democracy with a party, or Christianity with a religion, or man with profit, or God with idols.

Every time a man renounces of his own accord or is forced by others to renounce his creativity and his freedom to choose according to his conscience, the creativity of hope is dealt a sore blow.

It is only by working together, pooling all the potentialities of each and every one, that men can build something worthy of being lived by those who feel a vocation to the infinite and who are not content with a mess of pottage.

Every man is a creator and has the right to his own plot of ground, his own segment of time, in which to experiment with his creative power.

Every man is free and has the right of choice, not simply obeying the law but, above all, following the deepest demands of his conscience in harmony with the conscience of those whom he sincerely regards as being just and true.

Renouncing this, one's last dimension, out of laziness or denying it to others out of fear of losing one's privileges in the "disorder" caused by freedom, is to profane love and, consequently, to kill man, because a man may be stripped of everything else but he will go on being a man if he is allowed to exercise his freedom to love.

Man's last dimension is his right to be himself and no one else, the right to his own words, the right to his conscience, which cannot be replaced either by power or religion.

His last dimension is his thirst for existence and for creation; it is the urge he feels to come together with other men in order to build freely with them and not to carry out prefabricated programs which have been imposed on him by any spiritual or temporal power.

That ultimate dimension is what gives meaning to his whole life, for the sake of which it is worth his while to exist, to get up in the morning and to go to bed at night.

His last dimension is that minimum which is necessary for him to feel alive, to know that he is a person, one who has his own importance, to realize that he is a citizen of the world and fully capable of fidelity. It is that which, if it is missing, causes him to lose his identity and prevents him from acknowledging and accepting himself and from knowing the reason for his feelings and actions.

The last dimension is that which makes us see that others are as important as we, that there is not one time for loving and another time for suffering, that fidelity is not pain or sorrow, and that mere resignation is not fidelity.

The ultimate dimension which we call love without knowing what it really means, or which we call hope without knowing if we really have it, will always have connections with three irreplaceable realities: *freedom, conscience,* and *creativity.* These will be the key words of the following pages, which were written at a time in history when many people were feeling nostalgic temptations to turn to the past, while others were beginning to fear a resurgence of Fascism.

I'd like these pages to be a real contribution to the common hopes of those who are not resigned to seeing themselves deprived of the right to offer other men their own dreams, their own weariness, or the thoughts that they feel rising up within them.

I'd also like these words to be an act of faith in man's capacity to be reborn at a moment when everybody else is thinking about an apocalypse and the end of time.

I would like my words to be a gesture of hope, one that is partly polemical and partly innocent—a gesture of hope that, in spite of oppression and extermination, and even in the midst of our concrete jungles, flowers should go on blooming, love should continue to blossom, and that there should always be an olive branch to remind us that life goes on and that God has not yet repented of having created man.

I am grateful to everyone, both believers and nonbelievers, whose experiences have helped me to describe my own.

I dedicate these pages to "the last of all," who are the only ones who do not feel tempted to turn back, because they have no privileges to defend, and who always march forward even when we compel them to bring up the rear.

I dedicate this book to those who are "the last of all" because they are always the readiest for creative adventures and, consequently, the only true bearers of an undiminished hope.

1

Man in Search of Himself

Who am I?

This may seem a foolishly simple question, yet quite a few people today are asking it seriously of themselves. And, on the other hand, how many there are who arrive at the gates of death without ever having asked this question!

Nevertheless, a man begins to be a man only when he is capable of asking himself who he is.

The real drama of man begins precisely when he asks himself, "Who am I? Where do I come from? And where am I going?" and then realizes that he is only the product of others; that he has scarcely anything of his own, anything original; that perhaps he has never really thought for himself but has relied completely on borrowed ideas.

This drama begins when a man sees that he has been made what he is by political, cultural or religious ideologies, and that, consequently, he has no answer of his own to give to the great questions of science, religion and creation.

This is the anguish of a being who has been created

in and for freedom, but who spends his whole life without being able to live in freedom.

Man realizes this when he begins to see that he cannot be what he would like to be, since both his present and his future are in the hands of a few powerful people who run his life for him. It is then that he feels repugnance at living a life that has been prefabricated from elements he has had no hand in making.

And this happens even among Christians and those reared in a Christian culture, in spite of the fact that Christianity is a cry of freedom and creativity: "You have been called to freedom," wrote St. Paul of Tarsus, and he added elsewhere: "The word of God is not fettered."

Although the fight for freedom has been a hard struggle all down through history, it has reached it most critical point in the world of today. Fortunately, however, many people have begun to question themselves and to examine and not accept blindly the modes of life and action which others seek to impose on them from outside.

One of contemporary man's greatest discoveries is that it is more worthwhile to sacrifice one's life for one's fellows than for an idea or an ideology. The more blatant forms of crusading have been discredited, although the more subtle ones still go on.

In addition, man is beginning to see certain basic elements of his life in a new light—freedom, love, conscience, happiness, life, death, pain, sin, and eternity. Nowadays, the difference between the "old" man and the "new" is being assessed according to the value which each places on these eternal elements.

But just when men are beginning to discover their identity and to ask themselves decisive questions, they find that they have no satisfactory answers. Hence, if man, in his search for truth, is to arrive at a satisfactory answer, he must inquire among all of those who have succeeded in asking themselves what they are. This is not as easy as it seems because for all too many years the relationships between men have been gravely misused.

As a result, the whole of society has reached the point of being organized in such a way that there is no longer any real relationship between men; no longer is there that relationship which everyone truly desires but which most people today regard as unattainable because all the cultural possibilities of reaching it have been exhausted.

The fact is that we have learned to see in our neighbor not a friend, a comrade, an ally in the long adventure of life, but an enemy, a rival, someone against whom we have to defend ourselves and whom we may have to crush if he gets in our way. Hence comes the modern lust for power, because power gives a man the ability to defend himself better against others and provides him with the means to put them under his feet. And, unfortunately, man feels stronger and greater to the degree that he sees others weaker and smaller.

Even in religion, which should be the main liberating force, the voice of conscience, which should be raised against every crime committed by one man against another, has been, to a great extent, converted into an instrument of power, one of the strongest of such instruments since it involves man's deepest feelings and operates where he is most vulnerable and open to attack—the sphere of mystery and of death.

The liberating God of Christianity has been turned into the tyrant God of the different churches, and this has been one of the most harmful and most negative misfortunes that has befallen man in his long struggle for freedom.

God has been falsely and gratuitously represented as man's absolute master and not as his brother in all his weariness and hopes; He has been pictured as a tyrant who can dispose of our freedom as He wills, who can demand that we believe in the absurd without being able to rebel against it, who capriciously shapes our personal history and that of our world according to His every passing whim, selecting arbitrarily those whom He wishes to save and those who shall die. And the natural result of this is what we now see: the abuse of power in the very name of God.

If God is the master of the world, then becoming like God means becoming more "masterful"; hence, the more power one can achieve, the more grace one receives from

God, the more truth, the more right to meddle in the lives of others without being ashamed of doing so but rather boasting about it, since then one is "God's representative" and has been given the "grace of state" to subjugate others.

Hence those who have succeeded in acquiring authority, such as the personnel manager of a factory, the bishop or the father of a family, the professor or the eldest brother, may feel very pleased with themselves. And conversely, anyone who has no power over anybody else may not only feel that he is not a real man but also that he cannot be a real image of God. Therefore, it is not surprising that many of those who set themselves seriously to fight for man's complete freedom may have felt at one particular moment the need not only to abandon religion but to wage war on it as an active enemy of man's liberation.

It is only today, after the distinction between religion and faith has been made with great difficulty, that things are beginning to change to the point that many atheists have come to see that a living and dynamic faith is not an impediment to man's freedom but can even be an important contribution to that freedom. Many "new" Christians have paid for their commitment to the struggle for man's liberation by suffering poverty, imprisonment and torture, and this has led many former enemies of religion to view Christianity not in the light of a tyrant God but in that of a God who is the Son of Man, who came to destroy all racial barriers, all power directed against man, and all inequality between men and even between God and man. As Christ Himself said, "I do not call you servants but friends."

When men are presented with this image of a different God—one who sits down at the same table as they—they see clearly the need for new forms of civil and religious democracy, for a new kind of human relationship (both inside and outside the family), for a radical reappraisal of the nature of that family, the need to initiate experiences of community life never envisioned before as a permanent, free and creative dialogue with all men.

This new image of God makes possible a new human community, one which will be truly human only when every member of it finds therein the space and the freedom which will enable him to lose his fear and shame of communicating to his neighbors and to history what he feels within himself and which is his own, original contribution to others.

Becoming aware of the fact that the relationships between individuals, families, nations and peoples are in a state of profound crisis in spite of new attempts at reconciliation is the first step in a common search which has not been undertaken until now; it is the first phase of a new worldwide conversion and of a new image of man.

But this new image of man is not just a project of the future. One can say that it has, to some extent, already begun to appear. We can discern the first traces of it, either as a concrete reality or as an initial attempt to bring it about. Elements of it can be glimpsed in all fields of human endeavor, from the scientific to the religious, from the philosophical to the political.

This new image of man which is being timidly and painfully traced out is a proof of man's ultimate resurrection. It is a proof that he is still greater and stronger than any structure, than any planned extermination, than any alienation or tyranny, and than any of his preconceived images.

Moreover, for Christians it is the proof that Christ's death and resurrection were not in vain. It is a confirmation of the promise of the Revelation or Apocalypse of St. John: "I shall make all things new." It is good theology, for it assures us that men have already begun to rise from the dead and that they are always called to life even though the problem of death has not yet been solved.

It is confirmation that victory belongs to life and not to death even when we see death stalking the streets as a master among his subjects.

It is only by resolving, on a note of hope, the dialectic between life and death that man will ever be able to free himself from suicide and despair.

And this is true even when, as today, more and more men feel called to offer to their fellows the only part of their lives left to them, namely, the holocaust of their deaths, as their supreme gift or their last protest.

2

Creativity and Freedom

A man is not free if he is not creative, and no one can create if he is not free. Hence creativity and freedom go hand in hand.

To my mind, creativity is simply freedom in action as the expression of that which is original and genuine in oneself. The moment in which I create is precisely the moment in which I actualize my freedom. And by true freedom I understand the continual possibility of pronouncing my creative "Yes!", with no one to prevent me from doing so. Consequently, the man who succeeds in creating is the most dangerous for the established order and hence the most revolutionary, because he is engaged in a process of liberation which brooks no limits.

My freedom is real if it is born of a creative process, and creativity gives freedom its wings if it is the genuine expression of one's being, which strains toward freedom as the aim of all history; otherwise, creativity is false, since true history is nothing else than a continuous, all-embracing process of liberation.

Creativity cannot be defined once and for all, any more

than life and love can. Men have been living and loving for millions of years, but no one has yet been able to define love or life. Of course, thousands of definitions have been proposed, but this only goes to show that no one has succeeded in defining these great realities satisfactorily.

However, this does not prevent the men of each era in history from arriving at their own conclusions. If the process of liberation leads on to creativity, we can immediately see that it has done so and rejoice in it. But if that process remains in its spontaneous state, without finding the means to express itself historically, then freedom does not blossom but, as so often happens, remains inactive, and we suffer because it does so.

The history of man, which is the history of his creativity, since God Himself made man a creator, has been strewn with obstacles resulting from a lack of creativity and causing periods of slavery at every level—religious, cultural, political, economic and others.

Without giving in to pessimism, we must nevertheless acknowledge that we are at a moment in history in which, perhaps as never before, anti-creativity is being organized on all sides. The established order, because of its fear of everything new, is the tomb of creativity and uses every means, even the most Machiavellian, to nip in the bud every manifestation of a really creative spirit. If we forget this fact or do not take due cognizance of it, even the most generous of our efforts will be in vain and will be in danger of being used against us.

Therefore, although it will never be possible to organize creativity since to do so would be the most anti-creative thing we could do, we must be aware of the urgent need to find means that will allow creativity to be possible and prevent it from being suffocated by the worldwide organization of anti-creativity.

If anyone feels like mentioning Satan in this context, this is the place to do so because killing off creativity means burying the Gospel and Christ Himself with it.

And that is the only real atheism.

It is quite possible that we men of this generation are witnessing a life and death struggle which could stop for centuries to come the true process of human liberation.

Certainly man has a capacity for rising up and fighting against alienation, a capacity which is greatly superior to any organized slavery, so that, while history continues to flow on, man always ends up the victor. But we must not be ingenuous. Hope is not the same as ignorance, nor is resignation the same as happiness.

One can sense everywhere the reversal of that trend toward a new creative process of liberation which had begun to emerge, and this reversal could be fatal for future generations because it could stop the building of a new world for many years to come. And we cannot resign ourselves to building tombs even though we may be convinced that they will inevitably be reopened some day to allow creativity to rise once more in triumph.

We must make an effort to keep on finding new and better means of putting creativity to work, means which will be, to use the Gospel expression, the new wineskins needed to contain the new wine, as necessary now as they were twenty centuries ago. Let's take two concrete examples, one from politics and the other from religion.

In the realm of politics, we have had an evolution from absolute monarchy to enlightened monarchy; then from enlightened monarchy to constitutional monarchy; next, from constitutional monarchy to republican monarchy; then from republicanism to democracy; from democracy to socialism; and finally from socialism to a classless society.

Although the objectives of the successive steps of this evolution have normally not been accomplished, each step in that evolution has been more open and creative than the preceding one, and each required new means for its accomplishment. It is in acquiring these means that man's creative ability has shown itself: the success or failure of each project depended upon that ability.

Consequently, leaving detailed discussion aside for the moment, it is clear that these processes of history have always contributed something, a step forward or a greater degree of freedom. Whether the experiment succeeded or failed later on is another question. There is, however, no doubt that in the evolution from a republic to a democracy, from a democracy to socialism and from socialism to a classless society there has been an attempt at creativity and a search for a wider extension of freedom.

But there is a pitfall here. I am always doubtful of the creative abilities of those who think that, when one of these processes of evolution fails—say, for example, socialism—then the solution consists in finding a new means of realizing "true" socialism. To my mind, this would be a step backward, and hence it would not be creative. I believe that true creativity consists rather in finding some means that will permit us to achieve the next step in that socialism which would, for example, be the real human community capable of carving out its own future without relying on anyone else.

We must never be afraid of pushing forward. Human creativity is never exhausted, for it is infinite. Hence we must never sanctify any one method or means as being definitive and exclusive, for there will always be new possibilities of discovery. Let us now take an example from the religious sphere.

The council which Pope John convoked was a truly creative event in the history of the Catholic Church, as even the Marxists admit. It was a radically new element in the life of the Church. It was a tremendous step forward, a new broadening of freedom within the Church and even beyond it.

But why has this indisputable act of creativity been repressed to the point that it now appears to have been only a nice dream? Many people believe that this is due solely to the forces of reaction which have come together in order "to put things back in their place again." Actually, that is not the only element involved. We simply have not been able, or we have not had the courage, or we have not been allowed, to find adequate means to contain and foster the creativity that burst forth in the Church.

The true creative force of the council consisted in realizing that there had to be a revolution within the Church with regard to its mode of government so that it would no longer be pyramidal, from above downward, but that it should instead begin from below, from the people of God, the great silent mass along with their bishops; from the individual churches; and from the bishops of the various dioceses, in concert with the Bishop of the Church of Rome. In that way, a definitive break would have been made with the pyramidal, absolute monarchical structure which had killed the true creativity of the people of God and had obscured the real face of Christ the Liberator and of man as co-creator with God.

However, while the council itself was indeed creative, obviously the means employed after the council to bring about the great revolution have not been sufficient. Actually, what we have tried to do is put the new wine into old bottles to which we have merely given a new lick of paint; for example, no matter how we may have updated the Roman Curia, it still remains.

The Roman Curia is an instrument conceived and created for a pyramidal, and not for a community, form of government, for a church which rules by law and not by the Gospel. If we wanted to channel the council's creativity, we should not merely have "reformed" the Curia but found new modes of government, capable of giving life to the new course of the Church. Hence the enormous importance of the means employed in the dynamics of creativity.

If creativity is to be real, it is not enough for it to have spontaneity; it is not enough to have three or four Christians here and there shouting that the Pope must be elected by the people and not by the Cardinals; nor is it enough for a Belgian Cardinal to launch a few accusations against the Curia.

All of this can be useful and can be part of a world struggle, but it is not enough. Entrenched power is greater and stronger than spontaneous gestures of protest; power has in its hands old but well-tried means of defending itself against innovation. Consequently, we must have new methods if we wish to put creativity into action.

The truth is that Pope Paul had great intuition in this matter. I believe that he, too, understood to some degree the need for new instruments to put the spirit of the council into effect; and so, although he did retain the Curia, he began to create new organisms, completely original and with a fresh logic, totally different from the rigid, absolute structure of the Curia. These were centers for dialogue, unencumbered with power of any kind and entirely open to every form of initiative and creativity. I am referring, of course, to the secretariats for dialogue with other religions, with the separated churches and with nonbelievers. It has even been said that Pope Paul looked upon these innovations as a pledge of a new administration in the Church.

A system of government based on dialogue would certainly have meant the end of abuse of power and would have opened the door to self-rule within the Church. But in actual fact, Pope Paul's first encyclical on "dialogue" was badly received by the "old wineskins" of the Roman Curia, and the new organisms were too young or too frail to escape being swallowed up by the curial Colossus.

Thus, for example, the secretariat for nonbelievers, instead of promoting a real dialogue at ground level, as it were, has been turned into an instrument of dialogue at the top between selected personages. Now it is not the men who believe and those who don't believe who engage in dialogue, but only the different authoritative bodies. The secretariat has ended up being a forum for a dialogue between ideologies, promoting the politics of concordats and thus being turned into a useful instrument for those in power.

I am in complete agreement with the French Communist Roger Garaudy when he says: "The greatest revolution in the world is still to be brought about, and it would be a sin not to do it together." But I agree with him provided only that by "together" he does not mean to restrict the revolution to Christians and Marxists, because if he does, I am very much afraid that the whole thing will end up by being a dialogue between ideologies. The great revolution must be brought about by all those who are conscious that things have changed radically, who believe in the power of creativity, who accept man as the center of history and who cannot conceive that one man could abuse another in any way. If these provisos are granted, I shall ask no other credentials from anyone. Ideologies are what they are and cannot change. But we, individual men and women who are actually living now, can change. When we begin the process of dialogue and creativity, of searching for something completely new, all former identities will disappear. We are all human beings in process of transformation. When Garaudy was asked about his Christian faith, he refused to reply directly and said: "I am a man in search of the truth and struggling against oppression."

If a dialogue is begun once more at the level of ideologies and at the top, between Christianity and Marxism, we could arrive at the absurd position of reinforcing power instead of freeing men from its tyranny. The top echelons of every system are authoritarian and dogmatic; they are in favor of preserving order and are afraid of creativity.

I would look with fear on an alliance between the Vatican and the Kremlin. When I think about such an alliance, I cannot forget how the Gospel implies that Christ had to be crucified before Herod and Pilate became friends.

Consequently, although in the past a few men of genius and a few heroes were sufficient to ensure a minimum of growth in civil liberty for the people, and a few saints were enough to salvage the genuine creativity of the Gospel, it is quite clear that today the responsible participation of everyone is required if the process of common freedom is to be successfully worked out and that all the faithful must take part in proclaiming the word of God.

I think that the moment has arrived for the people of God to take His words into their own hands; but the church of power is afraid of liberalizing the preaching of the word of God. Thus a new document from the Council on the Liturgy forbids Christians to take the floor during liturgical assemblies.

This is a new despoliation, since St. Paul states that the word of God is not "fettered," that it is free and belongs to everyone. Actually, Christ gave it to the people and never refused to engage in direct dialogue even about the most important truths of the faith.

This is a fear that has become tyranny since it puts a halt to the process of liberation.

Until recent years, the word of God in the liturgy was spoken in a language unknown to the people. True, nowadays it has been translated, but it is still the exclusive inheritance of those in authority.

Young people especially feel that the Gospel must belong to everyone and that everyone should be able to "speak his piece" about it. And they feel this way because, on the few occasions when they have been able to do so, they have experienced the creativity and great novelty of the exercise.

Hence each person has to create for himself his own means of expressing and realizing himself in the community and of speaking in the Church. But at the same time it is evident that, with all good will, no one today can free himself by himself from the heavy reality of the old structures that prevent the development of creativity.

This, then, is a work that must be done together. The need for this search in common is one of the most characteristic marks of a younger generation that is vital and sincere, alert to the processes of liberation in the world.

This is why spontaneous groups, both in the field of politics and in that of religion, are most likely to be excommunicated from the system. In fact, the serious search, conducted in common, is one of the greatest and most dangerous revolutions because it makes creativity mature.

Therefore, in the name of this creativity, we must do everything possible to prevent the damping-down of the innumerable creative tensions beginning to appear here and there as the most tangible sign of the new hope that is emerging. It is urgently necessary for us to find new, concrete means of making creativity possible and thus prevent it from being killed off; otherwise, all our efforts, even the most creative, may be sterile and may even serve to reinforce anti-creativity.

One of the most important things in fostering creativity is that all of us, believers and nonbelievers, working together, should set out to discover what the deep roots of anti-creativity are.

For believers of all religions, this deep root is a false idea of a God exterior to man, set over against him as a master and a rival—an idea which ends up making it impossible to discover one's own freedom and originality, with the consequent denial of life for oneself and for others. This image of God conditions all our relationships with other men and justifies a kind of continued submission of slavery.

On the other hand, for nonbelievers, for those who live without God, the root of tyranny lies in the fact that a simple denial of a tyrant-God—and this could be positive —is not always accompanied by a sincere recognition of the mystery of their own origin. Instead of looking for the origin of life within themselves, nonbelievers often seek for it elsewhere, in absurd ideologies that attribute creativity to matter or to an absolute God, ideologies which, in the end, converge in the figure of the tyrant-God who impedes all true creativity. And this is where believers and nonbelievers join hands.

In the case of unbelievers, their mistrustful attitude toward others arises, not from the strictures of the tyrant-God of believers, but from their own unresolved mystery, from their existentialist confusion. The fact that they have not solved the problem or the mystery of their own origin causes them to suffer from a lack of profound unity within themselves, and they project this lack onto others and attribute to them their own confusion.

Therefore, when this anti-creativity has been identified in believers and in nonbelievers alike, the source of personal creativity common to both is plain to see: it is conscience. For believers, conscience is the meeting point of the divine and the human—the only place where man really meets God, that divine something which is more than man. There lies the first and supreme source of all morality.

On the other hand, for the nonbeliever, conscience consists in recognizing within himself a mysterious capacity for ever greater human endeavor, that which modern humanist Marxists call "man's being greater than himself."

This recognition of creative capacity, in which believers and nonbelievers can meet, is very difficult to square with the passive acceptance of ecclesiastical, academic, political, economic and juridical structures and institutions which man accepts as completely natural—as he still accepts today his own condition as a slave, under a heavenly or an earthly master.

Therefore, once a man has found the source of creativity in his own conscience, which no longer tolerates any master, it is necessary for him to find the means that will permit him on the one hand to overthrow the old institutional structures of society and, on the other, to open up new paths of creativity.

Here are a few ideas about some means which I consider indispensable for beginning this new search and realization.

The first means consists in guaranteeing the possibility of expressing and realizing directly one's personal sovereignty in all forms of social life, rejecting any type of external mediation. I am referring to the enormous effort that must be made in the area of power if creativity is not to end up in a tomb.

The second means consists in allowing men to work creatively and, consequently, to refuse any type of work in which they think they are being made to carry out a production project that has been decided solely by others, who thus make mere instruments out of them. In this sense, we shall never get away from the blackest slavery while work means productivity and not creativity.

Here, then, we are beyond the area of self-direction and participation and are striving for work-creativity; and if we cannot attain it, absenteeism would be preferable, because hunger is better than slavery.

The ideal is that man should be able to live without working; or rather, that man should not be obliged to work in order to live. Society should guarantee everyone his livelihood. Logically, those who are able to do so will have to contribute to community services, with no one being excepted. For example, everyone will have to give part of their time to sweep the streets or clean the factories. Meanwhile, each one will devote himself to work that is not a form of slavery and which he does, not to earn his living or because he has nothing else to do, but because it is really creative. Each one will engage in that work which he feels will fulfill him, make him more a man and give him a sense of his own existence.

And this is not impossible. Experts in the relevant fields assure us that it can be done, given the political willingness and the creative imagination needed to organize it.

Another important point: we must invent some freely available means of communication between those places in which people are working for the freedom of all men; a means of communication capable of neutralizing the destructive effects of the instruments for molding public opinion, from the most elementary, such as the traditional political club, to the most sophisticated and well-concealed publicity powerhouse; a means of communication that can combine all the movements towards personal and group liberty into one drive for a new community which will be open to the creativity of all.

The field of education is perhaps the one in which the greatest effort must be made to find new means of creativity, since little has been done there in this regard. We must find how to make the transition from the policy of "learning or repeating known facts" to that of "a search in common" so as to be able creatively to reach new dimensions of truth.

We must not forget that the mind of the child is always the least alienated and that it is the student and not the teacher who asks "Why?", which is the beginning of every sincere search. When we, the teachers, ask "Why?", it is for very different reasons. Every question asked by a child is much more creative than any question asked by a teacher.

Hence, the student should gratefully acknowledge the sacrifice which his teacher must make in accepting this handicap as a condition for doing his best work. Perhaps this is what Christ meant when He said: "You are not to be called rabbi" (Mt 23:8).

Finally, it will be necessary to throw down all those ideological and religious structures that have made man a product of other men or of things, whereas he should be the author and protagonist of his own fulfillment.

Only in this way can the creative possibilities of all men be realized. Only in this way can men have a new basis for hope.

Thus it will become increasingly clear that true creativity coincides exactly with the liberation of all men, and, consequently, that true human creativity does not exist unless it is committed to the liberation of everyone and not only of some, as the greatest expression of the total gift of oneself.

Only along these lines can creativity and freedom merge in the definitive dimension of love, a love that will always be creative, revolutionary and fulfilling.

Hence we cannot repeat often enough that, while even one man remains enslaved or hindered in the exercise of his creativity, we cannot consider ourselves free or creative but rather still committed to the struggle for freedom.

3

Freedom of Conscience

When I was studying the history of religions and seeking for the motives that urged me to accept a faith which other people had handed on to me, one of the most important discoveries I made was that the Christian religion proclaims quite categorically the primacy of conscience over external law.

Since then, my moments of greatest suffering have occurred whenever someone I know abandons his faith, convinced that it cannot be reconciled with fidelity to himself because, as Vatican II puts, he has been taught "erroneous doctrine."

I recall with grief a letter I received from a young friend of mine, a student of engineering, in which he said: "As a Christian, you can never live your own life with any real freedom because you will always have to wait for someone else to make up your mind for you. Your faith will inevitably affect any decision of conscience you'll make."

It is a sad fact that every passing day sees an increase in the number of those who, out of fidelity to their consciences, feel obliged to give up their religion—young people who believe that their religion hinders them from making their own choices in moral and political matters; women who think that it is contrary to their personal dignity to have a child they don't want; married couples who cannot reconcile the freedom required by their married love with certain demands of Catholic morality; good citizens who refuse to follow a religion that justifies the use of arms; divorced couples who have remarried and founded new families which they believe in conscience to be true expressions of love; scientists and writers who feel that their creativity is stifled by belief in a particular religion.

A friend of mine, an Italian priest, told me recently about a young mother who had had five children in six years and who had committed suicide by throwing herself out of a sixth-floor window, not because her husband had been "playing around," as the press put it, but because she had been unable to overcome certain guilt complexes created by a particular type of Catholic formation. Her dilemma was a simple one. She loved her husband deeply and did not want to refuse him; but neither did she want to have more children since she and her husband were poor and she was almost overcome with fatigue. Yet she couldn't reconcile herself to practicing birth control as forbidden by the Church because she was tormented by religious scruples, so much so that she had often said, "I'll end up doing something crazy!"

Can Christianity really be accused of not allowing its adherents to exercise true freedom of conscience in making the fundamental choices necessary in everyday life? We certainly cannot deny that, down through the centuries, the Church as a structure has often opposed the conscientious decisions of many people. The Inquisition remains one of the blackest pages in the history of the Church, and Vatican II felt obliged to ask pardon publicly for sins committed against man and his conscience.

But while this is true, it is also undeniable that the Church, in her official teaching, has never betrayed the fundamental creative truth that conscience is always above every external law and that the God of Christians will judge men according to their fidelity to their own consciences and not according to any external law.

Indeed, even the fiercest enemies of the Church have been unable to find a single official document of the Church's teaching authority denying this basic truth. All they have been able to do is point to individual cases in which the Church has sadly betrayed in practice her Gospel message. Hence what we need today is a greater knowledge of the primacy of conscience over the law and a greater fidelity on the part of Christians in putting this knowledge into practice.

We cannot deny that for a long time and for a variety of reasons this truth was overshadowed, and we cannot honestly assert that the ecclesiastical authorities were blameless in this regard since, at certain periods of history, churchmen stressed fidelity to the teaching authority of the Church in order to safeguard an overly rigid concept of obedience. But that is not the whole story; there is anothr factor. Much of this sad state of affairs was due to the confusion that had arisen between the biblical and the Graeco-Aristotelian concepts of conscience. For the Greeks, conscience was only a philosophical category and was the same as reason, whereas, in the Bible, conscience is God present in the depths of each man's soul, what we today would call "being true to oneself." Hence conscience is a gift that is given to every man and not to the intellectuals alone, just as the sun shines and the rain falls on the earth for all men, good and bad alike; for God is no racist.

It is the task of the Church, therefore, not so much to "form" conscience or "take its place," as to help men to rediscover it, to listen and be faithful to it.

In a well-known statement, Cardinal Newman declared that obedience to one's conscience, even when that conscience is mistaken, is the best way to reach the truth; and, before him, St. Thomas Aquinas held that every one of the faithful should be ready to be excommunicated from the Church rather than betray his conscience. This, too, is basically what the Fourth Lateran Council said: "Everything that is done against conscience leads to hell."

Each of these statements was inspired by the teaching

of St. Paul, who was a most obstinate defender of conscience as the supreme value for the Christian. He put his own teaching into practice when he publicly disagreed with St. Peter: "I opposed him to his face, because he stood condemned" (Gal 2:11). In fact, he states that every action that does not spring from conscience is sinful because, for him, conscience is a light that legislates for concrete actions and that has authority because it is guaranteed by Christ.

But the new element in St. Paul's teaching is what we can call "previous conscience"; that is to say, it is not a question of a light which, after each action, tells me whether I have done good or evil. For him, conscience obliges by itself and can impel me to perform an action because God is speaking in me through my conscience. This new insight revolutionized the whole field of classical morality. St. Paul interprets Christ's teaching in favor of each man's freedom of conscience: "The sabbath was made for man and not man for the sabbath," thus representing conscience as man's supreme guide in the use of his freedom.

So it is that in St. Paul the leap is made from the written law to personal conscience: "You have been called to freedom. . . . You are free. . . . The written code kills, but the Spirit gives life" (2 Cor 3:6).

For St. Paul, conscience is linked with fraternal love in accordance with the moral teaching of Christ, who placed love of neighbor at the center of His message; so that St. Augustine could sum up the Gospel simply by saying: "Love, and do what you wish!"

Moreover, this appeal to the inner life of man which was later called conscience appeared in Israel, especially in the prophets, much earlier than it was proclaimed by Socrates. But, unfortunately, after St. Paul's time and especially in recent centuries with the development of scholastic theology, Scripture scholars paid little attention to conscience (leaving to philosophers the task of dealing with it) so that paradoxically the word "conscience" came to be used more in non-Catholic than in Catholic circles.

However, Vatican II, influenced by biblical research, proclaimed anew, unreservedly and without equivocation, the primacy of conscience, even of an erroneous conscience. This is one of the most glorious pages of Pope John's council. Yet it is also one which many people have not yet thought important enough to emphasize and which others have, in practice, tried to push aside, thus depriving the Church of a truth which she has so often reaffirmed.

In reality, Vatican II took full account of St. Paul's teaching and reminded us that man finds the law, not outside, but within himself: "In the depths of his conscience, man detects a law which he does not impose on himself, but which helds him to obedience" (*Documents of Vatican II*, p. 213). This is a law which the Creator Himself has written in the heart of every man and for which, therefore, nothing else can be substituted.

This is where man meets God: "For man has in his heart a law written by God...; according to it he will be judged. Conscience is the most secret core and sanctuary of a man. There he is alone with God...." (*Ibid.*).

Like St. Paul and, after him, St. Thomas and Cardinal Newman, the Council was not afraid to assert that man has to obey his conscience even when it is erroneous: "Conscience frequently errs from invincible ignorance without losing its dignity" (*Idem*, p. 214).

Finally, the Council stressed the concept that the biblical and not the philosophical conscience is the real meeting place for all men since it alone speaks the only true, common and unequivocal language: "In fidelity to conscience, Christians are joined with other men in the search for truth and for the genuine solution to the numerous problems which arise in the life of individuals and from social relationships" (*Ibid.*).

I know that many people will say: "But we were never taught this clearly. We were told that all we had to do was to obey the Pope's encyclicals and the Bishop's directives, and that if we did so, at least we wouldn't go astray. But what you're saying seems like a different religion!" This is, indeed, what seems to have happened in all too many cases, and it would be unjust not to criticize severely the failure of so many clerics to teach the faithful this sacrosanct truth of the Christian faith lest they would become too mature and independent. However, we cannot forget either that laymen, with the usual perversity of humanity, have contributed to this abuse by their own fear of freedom.

Although men shout a lot about their right to freedom, they often prefer to be enslaved or dependent so as to feel more secure; and although they assert their right to freedom of consicence, they would rather have their chosen course of action approved by some external authority.

And this is not surprising because it is more difficult, although possibly more interesting, to have to decide for oneself in the solitude of one's soul than it is to be given a ready-made, tranquilizing answer that spares one the anxiety of perhaps being mistaken.

While I was writing these words, I had a striking proof of this. Some time previously, I had had a long talk with a young married couple about the problem of conscience, and they were very enthusiastic about the Christian teaching on the primacy of conscience. Yet just a few minutes ago I had an urgent phone call from them telling me that, according to their doctor, another birth would be very dangerous for the wife and that, as a consequence, she will have to sacrifice her unborn child. They wanted me to give them an answer that would set their minds at rest and relieve them of the trying task of facing up to their own consciences.

"Doesn't your conscience tell you what's right?"

"Yes, Father. But we're so afraid. It would be much better if you could tell us what we ought to do."

This fear is the very thing we must cure if we want to have a more adult Christianity and a Church that is capable of proclaiming the primacy of conscience without having to limit its scope because we're fearful of the traumas it may cause to the immature and to those who are frightened by their own responsibility.

God does not go back on His word. He has placed in our hands the wondrous yet terrifying gift of having to choose according to our consciences, and He is not sorry for having done so. All we have to do is have the courage to accept this obligation—or else cease being ourselves.

4

A Letter to Those in Power

It's not easy to write to you people in power because I know it's not likely you'll ever read my letter.

You don't like dialogue, and you relish criticism even less, but the thing that makes you really nervous is resistance from the people. And so you try to win the applause of the masses, no doubt because in your hearts you know very well that true power belongs to the people and that you have usurped it.

The Gospel tells us that Herod wanted to kill John the Baptist but didn't dare, for "he feared the people because they held (John) to be a prophet" (Mt 14:5).

Isn't this ancestral fear of the people which haunts those in power a sign of the unresolved conflict between the people, who correctly feel that power belongs to them, and those who, by force or guile, have stolen it from them and monopolized it?

In former times, everyone knew precisely who those in power were. But that's not the way it is today. Now those who really wield all the power are faceless and nameless, shadowy figures who move behind the scenes.

Or perhaps it would be truer to say that they do have a name, and that name is "Money"!

You think you have power, but you are really only puppets in the hands of these faceless, nameless manipulators. If you don't believe me, just try and see if you can act according to your consciences; see if you can honestly carry out the real desires of the people. I promise you it won't be long before you find yourselves out in the street, lost in that pitiable parade of the unfortunate who have no say in anything.

You, too, are the slaves of that anonymous power, but because you have made a privilege of your illusion of power and not regarded it as a service, you have thrown in your lot with that power and not with those who live in poverty and misery.

As a result, you know better than the poor themselves that it's money that makes a man really powerful today in the world, and so you strain every nerve to build up your bank accounts, even at the expense of others. And the people know this. Is it any wonder then that they only smile cynically when they hear you speak gravely about truth, honesty and justice?

It has been said that power is evil in itself, but this is not true. Power, like wealth or faith or freedom, is a means which the Creator has placed in men's hands to be used for their total fulfillment, which is love. It is only when these gifts cease to belong to everyone, only when they are usurped by a few to be used against the many, that they become evil and diabolical.

Power is a means for giving a fuller life to the whole Christian community; it becomes corrupt and sinful only when it is used as an end and not as a means. When power and authority are confused with each other, then all possibility of building up the true, universal, human community is destroyed.

Authority springs from conscience; and he who acts according to his conscience has authority even though he may never exercise it. The Gospel says of Christ that He spoke "with authority," because He spoke the most profound truth. Conscience is every man's greatest strength, and it is stronger than any power. The strength of a power that has become tyranny can conquer but not convince, whereas the strength of conscience does not conquer but does convince. Moreover, when you gain a victory, you lose a friend.

Although Christ was put to death by the ruling power, He remains stronger than all the powerful ones of the earth because the thing that really convinces is the voice of the conscience of all mankind. Behind the chains that now bind humanity, there lies a long history of freedom.

When you confuse power with authority, you are paying a big price for your ambition, because the most the people will do for you is either hate you or fawn upon you; but they won't love you. When you succeed in grasping power, you may be able to stand proudly erect with your foot on the neck of the weak and shout aloud your victory; but the moment you remove your foot, they'll sink their teeth into your heel. That is why you prefer law and order to prophecy.

But you must not forget, particularly if you call yourselves Christians, that the Beatitudes are still the manifesto of the oppressed and the writ of excommunication for the oppressors. You must remember that the real revolution in power does not consist in going from one master to another but in giving power to everyone.

Don't forget that what Christ began on earth was much more than a simple class struggle, for it was the complete abolition of every kind of discrimination since, in His revolution, the greatest had to become—and not merely call himself—the servant of all, which is the same as saying that there are to be no longer any "great" people or "little" people but just people.

And do not forget that Christ praised the unjust steward in the parable for his shrewdness in dealing generously with his master's debtors when he saw that he had lost favor with his employer and faced almost certain ruin and disgrace. In this way, the steward ensured that if and when he was dismissed from his post of power, he would at least not lose the friendship and goodwill of the poor.

Those of you who have power and are aware that it does not belong exclusively to you have a mission, the mission of being courageous enough to work so that power may begin to be shared by all and not remain yours alone; the mission of seeing that this power is so divided up that everyone participates in building up the community; the mission of truly standing beside those who do not have power and of being prepared, if necessary, to lose favor with the gods of commerce rather than deprive yourself of the friendship and the authority of the sons of God who are the brothers of Christ, the brothers of Him who made us all free. That is the only way that love can be spread on earth; and whatever does not carry within it the seeds of love is already Hell, even when you insist on calling it Heaven.

However, I suspect that you, too, are aware of the emptiness of your paper paradise. That is why you are unable to taste a moment of true, simple, serene happiness and why you really envy your chauffeur and his happy family life, even on the pittance you pay him. And you fear the conscience of the most miserable of your subjects, who, when your eye happens to fall upon him, reminds you like a judgment that the sun and the rain belong to everyone and not to you alone; although the poor are convinced that, if it were possible, you'd keep even the sunshine all for yourselves.

5

The Effort of Making Decisions

Young people, especially, are becoming increasingly aware that when we are faced with the grave choices inevitable in life, we cannot delegate our own responsibility to others. Our lives must be lived with the greatest respect for, and fidelity to, our consciences, which are always more demanding and stricter than any counsellor or moral theologian.

Yet, at the same time, young people experience great difficulty in exercising this freedom of conscience because, for the most part, their historical, cultural and family background is not receptive of this Christian discovery of the primacy of conscience over everything else.

Hence arise tensions and crises that are not easy to resolve. For example, the youth of today find it more and more difficult to reconcile their faith with that of their parents, so much so that one sometimes gets the impression that the two generations have different, if not completely opposite, ideas of the same God.

This was brought home forcibly to me recently when I was involved in a tense situation which was by no means

29

an isolated incident. Two young people were thinking
about getting married. However, about ten years previously, they had each become disillusioned with religion
and had ceased to practice it although this had not pre-
vented them from throwing themselves heart and soul into
working for political and social reform.

The girl's parents were of the old school and were hor-
rified at the idea of the marriage. It was bad enough
that she had stopped practicing her religion, but the fact
that she was going to marry an artist who had no religion
either was just too much for them.

"If only she'd marry a decent religious young man!"
they said, and did their best to stop the wedding; and this,
of course, only made the young people all the more deter-
mined.

Finally, the date was set for the marriage, and the
parents were sick with disappointment. In fact, the girl's
father had a heart attack, and the wedding had to be
postponed for a while. Then the parents begged for just
one favor: "Please get married in church!"

"But we don't believe in the Church!"

"That doesn't matter. At least, you wouldn't be dis-
gracing us publicly!"

This, naturally, posed a problem for the young couple.
They were being pushed, for merely social reasons, to
go through with a religious ceremony that violated their
consciences. At this point, the family doctor warned them
that the father might have another heart attack. What
were they to do?

There followed much consultation with priests who
were friends of the family. One "progressive" priest refused to perform the ceremony. "It would be a farce, a
mere comedy," he said. "I'd be an accomplice in a mockery of religion and acting against my conscience."

Another priest, a "conservative," after much thought,
could see no reason for such scruples, and concluded:
"Basically, you would, of course, not be going through
with the ceremony out of contempt for the sacrament."

In the end, the young couple, frightened by the doctor's
warning and anxious not to cause a family rift, went
against their consciences and very unwillingly got mar-

ried in church. True, they didn't receive Communion, but the parents did receive very happily and with no qualms, for the family honor had been saved. The young people could then go back to being atheists, if that was what they wanted. Anyway, they were going to live in another city, where no one would know them and where they wouldn't besmirch the family name.

At times like this, one is forced to ask oneself some questions. Are such parents really Christians, seeing that they used moral blackmail to compel their children to profane a sacrament? Can people really be Christians if they violate the consciences of others merely to save themselves a social humiliation? Are young people being honest when they go through with a religious mockery just to spare their parents' feelings? What is religious sensitivity? Does it mean that, even though you are not a believer, you feel pain when you have to make a mockery of a religious ceremony; or does it mean that you're happy when appearances are kept up even though you know that a sacrament is being profaned for that purpose? Should young people be true to their beliefs even when their parents' lives may be at stake? Is it right to give the sacraments to parents who force their children to commit a sacrilege?

It would be quite easy to find the answers to all these questions in any book of moral theology, but I don't think it would be quite just to do so. I must confess that I don't know what I would have done if I had been in that young couple's shoes. And so, when I was asked about the case, I hesitated to give a "specialist's" answer.

In my opinion, every Christian is a moral theologian when he truly makes an effort to live his faith in good conscience. And, indeed, so is every just man, whether Christian or not, who is faithful to the demands he feels deep within his heart.

When confronted with the dilemma of the young couple just mentioned, all I dare do is reflect that the heartache and pain, the scruples of conscience and the indignation they felt at being forced to act against their convictions, augur well for the future of their children. I'd like to think that it will be easier for them as parents to respect their children's mature decisions without complaining or getting heart attacks and even with the great joy of those who understand that man's most sublime gift is the exercise of his freedom. When all is said and done, who respects this freedom more than God, since He even permits us to act contrary to His will and commandments?

As an experiment, I presented the case of the young couple to people of different beliefs and backgrounds, and their verdicts surprised many "moral theologians" with their maturity and reasonableness. As one would expect, the verdicts were mostly concerned with the main characters in the episode—the parents, the priests and the young couple themselves.

There was almost unanimous agreement that the parents had acted more like atheists than like Christians, because, as a young Catholic worker remarked, "they rode roughshod over the young people's freedom of conscience and debased two sacraments, matrimony and the Eucharist." But, on the other hand, the father of a family took refuge in "sentimental" reasons and confessed to me: "I, too, would not have allowed them to get married in a civil ceremony. It would have been too painful for me."

Opinions differed more widely in regard to the two priests. Almost all said they respected the "progressive" priest's attitude in refusing to perform the marriage; and many, both parents and young people, approved to some extent the "conservative" priest's compromise as a gesture of "humanity" in the concrete, trying situation in which the young couple found themselves.

The reply of one young woman was characteristic: "If I had been in the same circumstances as the couple, I would have been very grateful to the 'conservative' priest, but I would have respected, admired and remembered the 'progressive' priest even though he had left me in a bind." Another girl, a medical student, said: "I've always thought that 'progressive' priests were the most liberal, and 'conservative' priests the most rigid. But now that I think about it, I realize that here the 'progressive' priest was, paradoxically, the more religious, the more faithful to his conscience and hence the more priestly of the two."

As regards the young couple's decision, opinions were even more divergent. Looking at the problem theoretically, many thought that the couple were inconsistent in going through with the religious ceremony; but from a practical point of view, they asked themselves if it wasn't more human and more Christian to spare the father another heart attack than to remain faithful to a personal principle.

A young Marxist student of philosophy said without hesitation: "They did the right thing. In their eyes, the wedding ceremony was not a farce because they simply didn't believe it was holy in the first place. For them, it was merely another traditional rite, like cutting the wedding cake."

On the other hand, however, a young working woman, also a Marxist, preferred to hold that "the young couple failed to respect a religious rite which, even though they did not recognize it as such, is still very important to many other people." But she laid the blame elsewhere: "The fault did not lie with the parents or the young couple but with society, with the bourgeois mentality, with a cultural tradition that has stifled the fundamenal principles of creativity and freedom of choice." And she added, "All of us must together look for new and better modes of living because we have all been born to choose and not merely to suffer our ways of life."

The importance of these new modes of life was demonstrated to me by the amazement of one mother who asked, "But wouldn't this mean that, in last analysis, each Christian could regard himself as a moral theologian? And then wouldn't we all fall into moral relativism, and everyone would do just as he pleased?"

Her daughter, a journalist, supplied the answer: "You have to be clear as to what man's fundamental values are. If you attribute a fundamental value to certain forms that are simply means for living out one's own faith, then rejecting these forms would be relativism. But in reality the fundamental values, which are freedom and love, remain untouched. And so, from this point of view, I think that the true Christian is he who respects, above all, the value of man's conscience, which, after all, is the basis for every judgment. In this sense, every one of us is a real moral theologian."

Who is right here, the mother or the daughter?

To my mind, the important thing is that a mother and daughter can discuss such matters freely, which is quite a new thing that cannot but be creative.

6

A Symbol of Conscience

There is an incident recorded in the Bible which is little known and which some people consider merely a tale for children. I'm referring to the story of Balaam's donkey, related in the Book of Numbers, which narrates the history of Israel's exile.

It seems to me that this story can have a very modern interpretation; the donkey belonging to Balaam the soothsayer can be regarded as a symbol of our conscience, so difficult to follow completely that we prefer to substitute external laws for it. In the Bible narrative we find: a talking donkey; a pagan soothsayer whom God turns into a prophet, making him bless what the king wants him to curse; an animal that is more faithful in following the road than is her master and that sees an angel before he does; a God, a man and a donkey who converse as naturally, spontaneously and innocently as children.

Such is the beautiful little story of Balaam's donkey, one of the most poetic pages in the whole Bible.

Is it a story for children or for grown-ups? For the stone age or for the space age? Has Balaam's donkey got anything to tell us about the secularization and structuralism of our modern world?

Since this is the age of liberty, real or imagined, everyone is free to choose his own answers to these questions. As for me, I find this little donkey more up to date than today's newspaper. I'm only sorry that the biblical author did not give this charming animal a name, because, so far as we can tell from the Bible, she is the only animal that God has allowed to converse with men since the time of the Garden of Eden. And I don't think Balaam will mind if, after so many centuries, I take the liberty of providing a name for his trusty little beast. I'd like to call her "Conscience." Every one of us can call her that, because we all came into the world bearing her within us.

Like Balaam, we are all convinced that we are more important than she is; but we forget that, if we act without her or against her wishes, we become animals, so wild that we are capable of saying "No!" to God Himself.

The way Balaam treated and spoke to his donkey is very like the way we speak and act with our conscience. We are well aware of its fidelity, and we even cherish it— provided that it doesn't rebel against our whims. But like Balaam with his donkey (Nm 22:29), we think our conscience is "making sport" of us when it is more faithful and more upright than our selfish maneuverings and won't allow us to drive it along false paths.

And then, as Balaam did with his donkey, we mistreat and insult our conscience, convinced that it's only having fun at our expense and that God couldn't possibly be talking to us like that. But just at that moment, God intervenes on behalf of our conscience, our "donkey," our faithful companion on the journey towards the light, making it speak forcefully yet with quiet dignity: "Am I not your donkey? Haven't you always been my master? Have I ever harmed you?", just as Balaam's donkey spoke to him (see Nm 22:28-30).

Can we not hear in these words of Balaam's trusty beast when he insulted and beat it an echo of our Lord's words on the eve of Good Friday when the soldier struck Him: "If I have spoken wrongly, bear witness to the wrong; but if I have spoken rightly, why do you strike me?" (Jn 18:23).

This story from the Bible is indeed very simple, but we should not disregard it, nor should we forget Balaam's donkey, a fitting symbol of our conscience, of the warm, friendly presence of God within us, a presence that is tender, faithful and tenacious, like everything that pertains to God.

Balaam, the weak, self-assured soothsayer who thought he was stronger and more important than his little donkey, is a symbol of all those who think they can justify their evildoing by beating their consciences when those consciences refuse to follow paths that lead where truth does not tread.

The story is a timely lesson both for children and for grown-ups. When, like Balaam, we are about to do something contrary to God's commands, we should look around courageously and with faith because the jealous God of the prophets, the God who is man's friend, will bare our wickedness and will make our conscience speak, even though it be through the mouth of a donkey, if that is necessary, or the lips of a child, or by means of a rock in the road over which we stumble, or the visit of someone we didn't expect, or a car that injures us on the highway, or an unknown person who speaks to us only with a glance.

While I often find myself agreeing with the ultra-secularists, I hope they will forgive me for thinking that God is able to speak to an animal and that He will not refuse to work a miracle so that He can offer us poor devils of men His last word of hope.

Such, for me, is the God of Balaam's donkey, the God who lives within us to make us discover what life really is, and who always walks one step ahead of us to keep us from getting irretrievably lost.

7

A Letter to Slaves

What is a slave? Are there any to be found today?

According to some people, slaves belong to a bygone era and are now found only in movies and novels since men are no longer bought and sold in markets like cattle.

According to others, everyone who is denied any of the fundamental rights of man is a slave.

According to religion, anyone who cannot control his passions is a slave. But sometimes a man's legitimate desires to taste the good things of life are mistaken for passions.

I hold that there are slaves who are really free men, and so-called free men who are actually slaves; that some are enslaved by force and others at their own wish; that men often fear that liberty is a slavery and so seek slavery as a protection and a better substitute for freedom.

The "slave traders" will be finally defeated only when no man tolerates his own enslavement or that of others; but many still abuse the freedom of others by taking advantage of the masochistic streak in all of us.

"It's better to be a rich slave than a poor free man,"

they say. "It's better to be a slave without any worries than a free man with problems." These aren't advertising slogans circulated by those in power but expressions of the instinct for protection that keeps nagging at each one of us.

One sign that we have accepted slavery is the constant hope that a messiah will come from another world to break our chains.

A sign of freedom is recognizing that the God of liberty lives within every man who has ever had the open choice between slavery and freedom. The only true Messiah in history, Jesus of Nazareth, came to reveal this truth and always fled when people tried to make Him a political savior who would miraculously solve the problem of slavery.

A second sign of slavery is the fevered defense of our possessions, material or spiritual: power, money, virtue, reputation, friendship, faith, security.

Another sign of freedom is having the courage to throw away the key so that everyone who wishes can enter our lives; to give away our shirt, too, when someone asks us for our jacket; to retain our dignity and not grovel when our possessions are threatened—because hope tells us that we are stronger than anything people can do to us; that we are rich when we possess nothing but hope; that we are just men only when we have lost our fear of being thought sinners.

A third sign of slavery is the fear of being left without God.

A further sign of freedom is the joy of knowing that people can take from us only what we want to give or are prepared to lose, since within us, as in every man, there is something which no one can commandeer and which is the one thing we really own.

Another sign of freedom is the secure knowledge that we cannot lose God since no one can suborn Him.

Christ was totally free, because He was never afraid of losing anything or of being lost.

There is only one danger in the world of freedom—the fear of giving.

In giving, one never moves towards slavery but always

towards liberation: "Give to him who begs from you, and do not refuse him who would borrow from you" (Mt 5:42).

It's enough that we own what we are giving away; that we want to give it; that he who is receiving it remains free; and that we are not slaves ourselves, because Christ tells us: "Do not throw your pearls before swine" (Mt 7:6), and because "if a blind man leads a blind man, both will fall into a pit" (Mt 15:14).

As I see it, Christ proclaimed the manifesto of free men when He boldly announced that "whoever would save his life will lose it" (Mt 16:25); and He condemned voluntary enslavement when He condemned the servant in the parable who hid his one talent in the ground for fear of losing it (Mt 25:24-30).

Freedom means possessing nothing so as to leave room for receiving everything. But possessing nothing means that what we call our own must really not be ours, and that we should not even feel that it is. We must never idolize anything or anybody, not even freedom itself, since unwanted chains are the greatest force for freedom.

Yet Christ, who announced to men their liberation from slavery, loved all slaves, of whatever kind, without bothering too much about being hurt by their chains. He loved them and came to them as a free man, refusing to accept tribute from the establishment, ecclesiastical or lay.

He condemned the Temple and rejected tyrants. He blessed only men and women and preferred them to the law and even to His own reputation. Out of love for them, He bore the accusation that He was a blasphemer, an atheist, a womanizer, a demoniac, a heretic, a revolutionary.

He accepted the risk of losing everything—the protection of the reigning powers, who condemned Him to death; the support of the people, who clamored to have a brigand released in preference to Him; the presence of His Father, by whom He felt abandoned; the gratitude of His apostles, who betrayed Him, or fell asleep or fled or denied Him.

Alone, powerless, without support, even without the breath of life, He still won the greatest of victories by conquering death itself. And since then, those who have discovered the sweet taste of freedom have only one enslavement to fear—the temptation to go on preferring slavery to freedom.

All who choose merely to defend their own crust of bread or small slice of life and don't want to get mixed up in their neighbor's struggle against slavery will be guilty, before God and man, of the tears of the last slave on earth. He who is willing to lose his freedom and even jeopardize his life so that there may be one slave less in the world can truly be called, as Christ was, "the son of man" and a son of His Resurrection.

But where shall we find those who are so free and innocent that they have lost all fear of slavery, sin and possible death? For these are the ones who, like Christ and with Him, will put an end to the last vestiges of slavery, whether voluntary or enforced.

8

Christ, a Free Man

Christ was not a prophet who merely preached freedom; He lived it and refused to be anyone's slave.

It's true that He paid dearly for His freedom, but this is precisely the reason why that freedom still benefits us today, for its creative influence on history endures.

If we are to understand the freedom Christ proclaimed and lived, we must know the Person of Christ. Yet this is no easy task, for He is not a theory or an institution that can be described once and for all, but a Person whom we must search for continually since He bears in His sacred humanity the reality of the infinite.

We can truly say that none of our findings about man or the universe exhausts their reality and that surprises await us at every turn in the path of life. But how much truer is this of the mystery of Christ, the God who became man once and for all.

What do we know about Christ? Much less than we have still to discover, for we have scarcely begun even to guess at what He was and still is.

The image we have of Christ will always be shaped

and colored by our individual faith and historical circumstances. Christ's eyes will be the same color as those that gaze on Him.

For those in power, His eyes will be those of a strong man.

For the downtrodden, they will, instead, be filled with simple, disarming hope.

For the churches, they will be the eyes of the Lord and Master, the eyes of one in authority.

For the man in the street, they will be the eyes of a brother or friend.

Ordinarily, what we love most about Christ is the quality we ourselves lack or do not want to lose, and it is difficult for us to love in Him His objective truth and holiness, although we are well aware of them.

Hence it is difficult to know Christ.

Of course, we do have the Gospels; but they have been too manipulated and used by those who, during the long history of Christianity, have felt that they alone held the copyright on the word of God.

And we also have the tradition of the Church; but along with tradition we have the whole sorry repository of human small-mindedness that has often shaped the face of Christ to suit requirements that were entirely mundane or blatantly angelic.

People used to think that, if they knew God, then they knew Christ, too. But today we take another route, the discovery of man—not, however, a mere anthropological but rather a global discovery of his hidden thirst for fulfillment, the most secret urgings of his conscience, the voice of creativity not yet silenced in his heart, and his innate desire for God not yet completely extinguished by all the pagan conditioning that constantly bombards him.

Christ is the answer to all of man's hopes and the satisfaction of all his needs; the only complete Truth in history; the only truly free man; the first one in the history of mankind who not only proclaimed freedom but lived it without succumbing to the temptation of power.

He was the first one capable of uniting in the same life the human and the divine, time and non-time, earth and heaven, present and future. Man will discover God, not by *imitating* Christ, but by accepting the paradox of living like a man in order to become like God, for Christ was not a man who became God but God who became man.

It is becoming clearer each day that any search for God must proceed through man because, if the mystery which is man is abandoned, then the Christian concept of God will make no sense. Hence a search for the freedom of the Gospel must also proceed through man and his liberation.

Perhaps one of the things most needed for a deeper insight into Christ and into the freedom that He lived and proclaimed is the removal of certain ideas about God that have deeply conditioned our image of Christ. Fortunately, the idea that God is a monopoly of Western culture, a God that never really existed, is finally dying.

This is one "death of God" that doesn't lead to atheism but brings us closer to the God of the Bible: the God who is not in competition with man since He made him His co-creator; the God who cannot be neutral because He is the God of "Yes" or "No"; the God who, every time He meets man, must shake him up since He demands to be either embraced or repulsed.

He is the God, not of fear, but of awe; not of justice, but of truth; not of the privileged classes, but of the downtrodden; not of compromise, but of risk.

He is the God who brings a liberation of man that can never be personal only but must also be political or community-centered; the God who, from the start, taught man to defend his freedom.

Indeed, even primitive peoples had to fight for their freedom, of which the essential sign is the right to freedom of speech, while the aim of the struggle by the various forms of democracy has been to obtain ever greater guarantees of this freedom of speech.

All through the Old Testament, freedom is seen as a great gift. Moses' long march to bring his people out of Egypt was simply a flight from "the house of bondage" (Ex 13:3) to the land of freedom. But the Jews had to pay for their freedom with continual uncertainty, hunger and poverty, and so they were often tempted to return to the material comforts of slavery, which many of them preferred to the hardships of freedom.

And this temptation is still with us today, as can be seen from the way one section of the working classes has betrayed the others by accepting some forms of slavery so that they can continue to enjoy more material comforts.

Among the Hebrews, slaves were better treated than among other peoples. Moreover because of the law of the sabbatical year (Dt 15:12-18), slaves had to be set free at the end of six years and allowed to take all their possessions with them. And here, too, there were many betrayals by those in power trying to abrogate this law to the detriment of the poor. In fact, when Christ said that He had come to proclaim a sabbatical year, almost no one knew what He was talking about (see Jn 8:31-59). And we don't know much better today.

At most, the Church offers us indulgences; but perhaps people would pay more attention to what she says if she occasionally renounced all her possessions and removed all the merely church laws that are smothering so much creativity.

In the Old Testament, man's free will was clearly the basis of all responsibility. The prophets acknowledged this and continually urged the Jewish people to use their free will properly.

Christ so respected the free decision of His people that He submitted to the cross rather than compel Israel to accept His message of salvation. Thus He was far removed from the inquisitions that His followers would later invent in His name.

Luther denied free will, but even modern pagans know that they are responsible for their own decisions.

Christian freedom is new, not because it is different from true freedom, but because it introduces three new elements—freedom from death, freedom from fear and freedom from the Law.

We know that Christ came to bring freedom to the oppressed. Yet the Bible gives no definitions of freedom; it is not a treatise on philosophy but simply presents us with acts of liberation. The symbol of oppression in the Bible is Pharaoh, and God's efforts on behalf of His people consist in saving them from him.

True biblical freedom is always total; it is both internal and external; and we realize how difficult it is to attain this freedom when we see how much trouble God had in bringing His people to it, for they insisted on confusing it with national triumph. On the contrary, true freedom begins where the other man's freedom begins, and not where it ends. There are people who feel free only when they see slaves all around them; but the really free man feels that he's a slave as long as any other man is in bondage. It is an illusion for Americans, for example, to say they are free if they are not concerned about the freedom of Spaniards, Vietnamese, Poles or Greeks.

Isaiah prophesied precisely what Christ's mission was to be: "To let the oppressed go free, and to break every yoke" (Is 58:6). The freedom which Christ brought us is not a philosophical freedom, not the freedom of the Stoics, which is reached without personal effort. The freedom of the Gospel is not mere "holy indifference." It is a freedom born of love and faith in Christ, who freed Himself and became a liberator, not by committing suicide, but by allowing Himself to be killed for defending life.

True freedom is that which made St. Paul say, " 'All things are lawful for me,' but not all things are helpful" (1 Cor 6:12), because I must consider other people; because I cannot exacerbate the feelings of those who are still enslaved; because I cannot blithely scandalize the weak; and because my love obliges me to respect the development of other men.

Christ condemned every attempt at oppression when He excommunicated the rich and powerful; when He unmasked the so-called guardians of the truth, calling them hypocrites and accusing them of placing on other men's shoulders burdens which they did not lift a finger to lighten; when He accused them of ranging over sea and land to make a single convert, and when they had converted him, of making him a worse slave than themselves; when He allowed Judas to remain by His side until the final betrayal; when He respected the dignity of each man and accepted each one without discrimination.

And Christ proclaimed freedom when He preached the

Beatitudes, teaching that freedom consists in ceasing to adore idols and in laying aside arms, which tempt us to injure others; when He announced that victory will belong to the weak and to those who possess nothing, because only they are strong who have nothing to lose or who are not afraid of losing what they do have.

It is precisely for this reason that all the tyrants of history, from Herod to Hitler, have been deeply afraid of the enslaved, the weak, the free.

9

Does the Religious Life Have a Future?

At present, there are about a million and a half men and women members of religious orders and congregations, but this number is dwindling at an alarming rate because many are leaving and the stream of vocations is drying up.

Why is all this happening?

The easiest answer is to say that it is due to a lack of faith, the absence of the spirit of sacrifice or a loss of sensitivity to the things of God. These may be valid answers, but they are not the whole story, and other causes for the crisis must be sought.

We must ask ourselves honestly and without panic whether we today have a clear idea of what "the religious life" means and, above all, what the religious life means for the people of our times. In discussing this question, a modern Catholic writer has remarked that it will be necessary to "re-invent" the religious life. But isn't this the same as saying that the religious life, as we know it, has no future? Indeed, many sincere people are now asking themselves if this is not so. As for me, I believe that the religious life is now in a crisis of life and death.

The Superiors General of the various orders and congregations realize this and have urged the Holy See to permit them to experiment and explore new avenues of approach.

The fact is that it is no longer possible to offer motives to justify the religious life without posing certain fundamental problems which are not the mere imaginings of a few venturesome religious but which are, instead, thorny questions that bedevil many General Chapters on renewal.

Some of these questions are:

Do we have a theological definition of the religious life? We know that Vatican II has given us a document on the subject, but it is largely the result of compromise and bids fair to be the least regarded of the conciliar decrees.

What is the essence of the religious life? If we say it's a consecration that allows us to live fully our baptismal commitment, then we are well on the way to admitting that the religious life in its present form is only a means and not an end, for isn't the fullness of the Gospel life open to every baptized person and can't it be lived in any station of life?

Is consecrated celibacy the essence of the religious life? If we conclude that it is, we are closing the door on the new forms of religious life for married persons that are beginning to appear and against which the new theology has no objections to offer.

Is it community life? But then we have to confess that community life exists more vigorously and with greater commitment and intensity in many spontaneously formed communities outside the classical, official structures of the religious state.

Are the three vows of poverty, chastity and obedience the essence of the religious life? If they are, then we cut off at the root a whole new spiritual theology that has begun to ask whether or not poverty and obedience, for example, are truly evangelical counsels capable of being the foundation of a truly religious life.

The truth is that we have an abundance of "spirituality," including some very classical material, but we almost completely lack a true *theology* of the religious life, just as we lack a true theology of married life.

If we take the religious life as meaning the free choice of a concrete way of living the Gospel, then every form of religious life, present or future, is based on man's essential right to choose freely the way of life that will help him live the Gospel most fully. Hence, basically, the motives for choosing the religious life are the same as those for choosing any other form of life, such as the married state, for example. If we like, we can call these motives different charisms or gifts, but without giving a monopoly to the religious life.

I believe that we have outgrown the idea that a vocation, a special call, is necessary for the religious life and not for marriage. Even further, I think that a greater vocation is needed to form a family in fidelity to the Gospel than to live as a consecrated celibate in any form of the religious life. I do not mean by this that such a vocation is needed merely to procreate or to have a sexual encounter but that it is needed to form a real family— two very different things.

A serious study of the origins of the classical religious life would help us in our quest for answers to present-day problems, a quest which frightens many people but which is essential and must precede any study aimed at "reinventing" the religious life.

One question that must be asked is whether the religious life may not have arisen in the Church as a "supplementary state" to provide something that was difficult or impossible to find in practice within the ordinary Christian community. I realize that here I am touching on the basic reason for the existence of the religious state as a form of life distinct from that of the ordinary Christian. But the question must be posed because, as the ordinary Christian life matured, it was observed that the fundamentals of the religious life were being practiced, sometimes more genuinely, by those sections of the Christian community that lived their faith to the full.

For example, take the poverty practiced by so many

Christian lay groups as a witness to the hunger of the Third World and as a demand of the Gospel, a poverty that is more real and more visible than that of most religious "by profession."

Take also the theological concept of obedience in such groups as a search in common for the will of God, the one Lord and Superior, in the light of the word lived in the Eucharistic celebration.

Think, too, of the new dimension of a sexuality born of love and seeking to communicate at the deepest levels, passing from the concept of simple pleasure to that of a true liturgy of love based on the biblical idea of marriage as an image and realization of the union of Christ with His Church.

In view of all this, the guidelines for the renewal of existing religious communities will have to provide for the future of the religious life as it will emerge from the theological and historical processes to which it is being subjected today. Such a renewal must show the greatest respect for those who have already freely accepted and are living joyously and fully a form of life to which they have a perfect right.

But we cannot and ought not close our eyes to the plight of many religious in this period of transition. Some are suffering the agonies of death when they see how the new tendencies are threatening to disrupt their whole life-style of sacrifice and sincerity, and offering them instead a future that seems to betray their original vocation.

Others have lost hope after a long and painful struggle to change the structure of their institutes, and they feel that they are now incapable of opening up new paths which formerly they would have undertaken confidently and joyfully.

The direction renewal will take must not be decided without sincere, open dialogue with all the religious and with the ecclesial community in which they work so that everyone can search together for new ways in an endeavor to render real service to the Church. Moreover, these new lines of approach must be sought with true freedom of spirit, without prejudices or taboos of any kind, and with great fidelity to the word of God interpreted in the light of the new era.

A large part of what we today call the religious life belongs in fact more to the outward form than to the basic elements of that life. Thus the field of renewal can be very wide if we are not afraid to venture beyond traditional, nostalgic ideas, and if we take the decrees of the Council and the Holy See as starting points and not as the goal of the infinite possibilities of renewal.

The history of the Church teaches us that in the past there have been forms of the religious life which, in spite of the fact that they produced many saints, are no longer allowed in the Church. Therefore, why be afraid that many of the present forms of religious life may have to disappear because they have fulfilled their function and may, as a consequence, no longer be acceptable to the Church? We must be careful not to make too many things sacred which perhaps are more the products of history than special charisms of the Holy Spirit.

Whatever the concrete form the religious life may take in the future, I believe that renewal must be pursued according to fundamental principles that have already emerged from the sincere attempts at true renewal that are now being made (but not always with sufficient understanding and foresight on the part of the authorities).

A form of religious life based solely on "personal sanctification" is inconceivable at the present day. In order to be true to the Gospel, the religious life, whatever form it takes, will always be a means of living more fully our baptismal commitment, whose characteristics of self-sacrifice and service to mankind, especially to those most in need, are required by the soundest theology.

The renewed religious life will have to be in some way a radical reply to the "anti-world" and "anti-history" elements so prevalent today. By its very life-style, it will have to oppose the false values on which the new paganism of contemporary man is based.

Furthermore, the religious life in all its future forms will have to be in some way a decisive rejection of the thirst for power, of any manipulation of men, of the narrowness of a consumer society, of sexuality separated from love, of individualism, and of all forms of personal or community alienation. And it must be prepared to take the inevitable consequences that any real opposition to an unjust system entails—risk, insecurity, unpopularity and loss of privileges.

The religious of today cannot stand aside and refrain from giving public testimony, as individuals and as communities, to the values of the Gospel. It is inconceivable in modern times that any communities should exist whose members live in personal poverty in order to enrich their institutes. Such communities would betray the Gospel and the very essence of the religious life.

The religious life will have to make visible in some fashion the characteristic signs of the eschatology, that is, of the new world about which all men dream in their hearts. It will have to prove to the world: that it is possible to govern oneself without having someone wielding power over the consciences of others, and this can be done solely by the force of love and the common search to find God's will for the community and for the individual religious; that religious can live in a community which, instead of smothering them, helps them to be more free and to fulfill themselves better in all their dimensions, a community that is prepared to forego everything—efficiency, wealth, prestige, etc.—rather than sacrifice a single one of its members; that they can live and be profoundly happy, even on the human plane, without being rich or wanting to be; that it is possible to assist in the maturation of history and to commit oneself to every real demand of justice, even at the risk of one's life, without hating anyone, without losing faith in mankind, without using anyone and without feeling oneself alienated by belief in God; that renouncing married life does not mean renouncing the fundamental vocation to love—that, on the contrary, he who makes this choice can love more, can widen the sphere and possibilities of love and have a concrete, true love that does not exclude the most profound dialogue with one's fellowmen, even when one must renounce certain specific dimensions of human love in favor of a more universal love, a renouncement which, however, is not necessarily greater than those demanded, on another plane, by other types of life-style such as marriage.

The religious will have to show, by his emotional maturity, his life rich in human serenity, his joyful devotion to the welfare and happiness of others, that true love does not have to involve sexuality even in its noblest form, in marriage.

He will have to show by his deep commitment to his chosen way of life and by his joy in living that his vocation is as normal and as possible, as rich and as fruitful, as any other form of life. This will be the source of his prophetic power and his real testimony to the genuineness of his vocation.

Today many thoughtful persons are deeply convinced that the classical structures of the religious life are in a state of great crisis and that these structures must be developed along new lines, the most evident signs of this being, as we have already indicated, the loss of many religious (sometimes the best), the lack of vocations and the desperate efforts that sincere religious are making to find new paths of renewal to follow.

10

Communal Groups in Crisis

The fact that a crisis has occurred in communal groups does not mean that all hope for them is lost.

Today more than ever before we must not allow ourselves to be afraid of things that change too rapidly for comfort. We certainly are living at such a pace that today's solutions to yesterday's problems are of little use to us. Scarcely have we found the answer to a serious question than we immediately realize that it is incomplete and insufficient; and then we easily become disquieted and disillusioned.

Is it perhaps an inescapable feature of all man's searching that he can never plumb the depths of things?

An outstanding example of this inability to find a complete answer to a problem is the failure of the so-called "communal groups" which were set up as an alternative to the traditional family to achieve two purposes: first, young people wanted to put into effect their new awareness of the value of freedom and open communication; and second, they wanted to overcome the growing difficulty of developing and appreciating these values in the closed, possessive atmosphere of the family.

These new modes of life sprang up like mushrooms everywhere and were greeted with cries of gladness or groans of exasperation. They came in all shapes and sizes, from "communes" practicing complete sexual freedom to communities with serious political or religious commitments. But they were all immediately branded as hotbeds of subversion and revolution and were condemned almost en bloc by those sections of society that are always afraid of complications. This was a trying experience for the young people, who were consequently obliged to set to work and build their communities in the face of practically universal opposition and misunderstanding.

Today, after being in existence for some years, the groups themselves confess that they are facing a crisis. Disillusionment and bitterness have arisen in many of them, while others don't even try to hide their nostalgia for the past.

Were their critics right all along, then?

In my opinion, no. Right is always on the side of those who, whether young or old, do not surrender in the face of difficulty but go on searching tirelessly, who are not content to settle for what others have done and who want to shape their own lives.

But why is there now a crisis among the "communal groups," and why so soon?

The following is an analysis of these questions which we made along with some young people whose plans met with shipwreck and who wanted to find out the reasons for their failure.

First, many of these groups began, not as sincere quests for something new and for greater maturity, but simply as a rebellion against the authoritarianism of parents, as a flight from loneliness, as an alternative to the fear of not being able to stand on their own feet in a hostile world, or as therapy for personal problems that were often just the result of emotional involvements.

Then there was a basic lack of a true desire to inquire into the idea of "community," which was often confused with the concept of common life, or team work, or group therapy.

Finally, they frequently forgot that a real community group cannot be greater than the universal community, whose ultimate aim is an encounter with all men, not on the level of ordinary society, but on the *community* level as such or, rather, on the level of communion, of personal communication.

If young people are searching for a greater degree of personal freedom and reciprocal human communication as an alternative to their essential personal solitude, then the means they use, including the communal group experiment, will be valid only to the extent that these means help towards attaining freedom and communication—an obvious statement, but one whose truth is often overlooked.

Many experiments in community failed because they carried over to their new life in the group the old patterns and failings of the traditional family: loss of personal freedom, the boredom and monotony of common life, the lack of give-and-take, a more or less "charismatic" authoritarianism, and the subtle manipulation of the individual members.

If the community groups, as well as the family, are in a state of crisis, it is not because they are bankrupt in themselves, but rather because they are often simply bad copies of old patterns. We must not forget that "communal groups" are a new experiment that is being carried out by people who are indeed young in years but whose culture and traditions are age-old.

But the important thing to remember is this: it is only the means chosen by the young people that have failed and not their objective, the search for greater freedom and better communication. In fact, although the group experiment has largely come to nothing, few of the groups involved have stopped believing in the intrinsic worth of the values they sought to put into practice.

Hence, if the young people wish to come out of the crisis without being overly pessimistic or bitter about their failure, they will have to see that an alternative to a form of life that does not satisfy them cannot be found as if by magic in the creation of a community group and much less in merely getting together to share common life.

Their best alternative lies in adopting a different attitude towards other people.

Let's explain that. Up to now, the attitude of most people to their fellowmen has been to try to get the beter of them. But now they should seek and respect freedom both for themselves and for others. Up to now, couples have had to lock themselves into a shared solitude in order to find and communicate with each other. But now they must become aware that communication with each other or with their group can grow only if they are open to everyone else.

In short, we can say that the group is in a state of crisis because there is a crisis in the attitude which each of us adopts towards everyone else. Hence the search for something new is still open and is still valid, even though the means that have been used so far have not always been suitable.

Yet the means still available for this search continue to be almost infinite. And herein lies our greatest hope.

11

A Letter to Pessimists

I'm writing to you pessimists because we're living at a time when pessimism is spreading like a virus through all sectors of society—politics, religion, art and culture.

Many people regard pessimism as a temptation and suffer keenly when it assails them.

Others look upon it as a virtue and are rather proud of it.

But most simply accept it as inevitable and resign themselves to it.

I must confess that I view it as a dangerous sickness with which, to some degree and in one form or another, we are all infected, for the sources of pessimism lie deep in all our hearts and spring from our ancestral fears:

> our fear of losing what we have and of not getting what we want:
> the weak man's fear of the strong man's violence:
> the strong man's fear of the weak man's revolt:
> fear born of mounting disappointment and unexplained mysteries:

fear of the whole world outside, a world that is sometimes seen as concentrated in Big Brother's face:
and fear of nothingness, that oppresses the soul like
the silence of a cemetery.

There is no doubt that we are more strongly inclined
towards pessimism than towards optimism. But both are
temptations.

It is easier to succumb to pessimism because, although
we always desire happiness, our happiness is always on
the other side of the mountain and we must scale the
heights to reach it. In the Gospel, too, we find that Christ's
moments of pain, sorrow and anger are more numerous
than His outbursts of joy.

But while the temptation to pessimism is the easier
to give in to, it is also the more dangerous because it is
a hindrance, an evasion and a justification for our un-
acknowledged laziness. It is the most subtle, the most
graceful and the most devilish way of shutting ourselves
off from hope. Pessimism saps the strength of every human effort, snuffs out every spark of creativity and
smothers the first sign of revolt. Pessimists have never
thrown a scare into those in power; and they are the
favorite victims of oppressors.

But it is also true that, although most revolutions
fail due to pessimism, they really come to nothing because
they are staged by optimists, whom those in power still
fear less than they do the pessimists. However, the cure
for pessimism is not optimism but realism, for optimism
is simply the other side of the coin of pessimism.

The pessimist cannot see the clear depths of the river
still flowing beneath the garbage floating on the surface.
And the optimist is in danger of forgetting that the garbage is really there and that, if he doesn't clean it up quickly and efficiently, it will pollute the whole river, right
down to the botton.

Outside the back door of most houses stands the garbage can, and at the end of each day it will be more or less
full, depending on the number of people and the amount
of activity in the house.

When the pessimist sees the debris piling up in the

house, he feels tempted to ask, "Why bother to clean the place? It'll only get dirty again!"

And the optimist thinks, "What difference does a little more clutter make?", and lets the stuff accumulate until it almost crowds him out onto the street.

The realist, however, says: "It would be nice if we had no litter or garbage, but since we do have it, the best thing to do is take the trouble to remove it every day." And if he sees the amount of debris increasing daily, he knows that it could be the result of negligence or that it could well be because each day brings an increase in work, living, friends or a harder struggle for existence.

The realist never gives up the fight, with the excuse that everything will return to normal if he just leaves well enough alone, or that every revolution is bound to fail sooner or later, or that every joy must finally end in tears.

The realist sings a happy song even when his heart is heavy.

The pessimist sings, too, but he only sings the blues.

The optimist is always singing and for the life of him cannot see why everyone else shouldn't be singing as well.

Pessimism cannot be realistic because if the hope in our hearts had not been strong enough to overcome all our disappointments, then the whole world would long ago have been as dead as a morgue and suicide would have been the normal course for every intelligent person to take; and we would not continue to mourn when someone we love dies, and we would no longer burn with indignation when we see human rights trampled underfoot.

The increasing number of conscientious objectors, the indignation that people feel at seeing democracy degraded, the widespread fear that totalitarianism will take over, the ordinary man's desire for law and order in the face of the rising crime rate, and the gradual downfall of the ruling classes—all these are signs that men everywhere are looking for peace and freedom. And they want this peace and freedom despite their own contradictory habits of laziness, uncertainty and fear.

Christ said, "I have overcome the world."

But He also said, "They will persecute you."

I cannot imagine Christ being pessimistic, despite His

having sweated blood and having drunk the chalice of disappointment, doubt and despair.

Nor can I imagine Him as an optimist, even though He said that we can even move mountains with just a little faith.

Instead, I see Him as a realist: one who hoped against all hope; who died with a loud cry on His lips, not surrendering to death; who often sang in tears, but who *did* sing. And He goes on singing despite the fact that many of us, His disciples, don't know whether to laugh or cry.

He continues to say to all the pessimists of history: "Men of little faith, why are you afraid?"

And to all the optimists: "Watch and pray, because evil, far from being dead, still sits down at the same table as goodness."

And to the realists: "Be as innocent as doves but as wise as serpents."

12

The Unknown God

Although millions of good men still do not know that God exists, yet at the bottom of their hearts they are convinced that they have been called to become God, and so they feel a compelling urge to bring about the death of the Christian idea of God. Thus the aim of atheism has always been to kill God in a desperate attempt to make man God.

But was it not this very God, the God whom atheists do not know, who revealed to men that they are indeed called to be God?

Some will object and say: "But this is no unknown God. He's only the Christian idea of God!"

Yet although our God has revealed to us Christians that we have been called to be God, I'm inclined to think that even to us He is still an unknown God.

In the Areopagus, St. Paul announced to the Athenians that their unknown God was the God who had conquered the grave and had enabled man to find an answer to death. Paul's preaching on God was real and meaningful, but it did not express the whole idea of God, because men need a God who can give an answer, not just to death, but to life as well, because it is in life that men must discover and realize themselves.

Rising from the dead is meaningful if we know beforehand what life is and what it means for us. Death, too, is meaningful if we know beforehand why it exists and where it leads to.

And God will be fully relevant for us only if we know what we ourselves are.

Rising from the dead is not important in itself if we are not aware of the meaning of life. Many people do not want to rise again and are not interested in the Christian mystery of life after death. They prefer not to go on living after death because they have not yet discovered the meaning of life here on earth.

God will be relevant for men if He is the God who not only raises the dead but who also reveals to men that it is possible to believe in life and that real life can begin here and now.

God will be relevant for men also if He is the God who makes it possible for him to have faith, not so much in Him, but in themselves and in their fellow men. Incidentally, believing in God is easy even for those who deny Him, since men need God so much that, even when they reject Him, they make other "gods" for themselves.

As long as we do not have the courage to accept the Christ who came to reveal life to us and to assure us that life has already begun and that *we* are life, we shall find ourselves without an answer to life and we shall be satisfied if we can just find an answer to death. But this would really be no answer at all since we cannot give meaning to death without first discovering the meaning of life.

When unbelievers ask us, "Why God?", we usually give answers that do not convert them but only make them more convinced that God has to disappear if the question "Why Man?" is to continue being asked.

Today more than ever it is clear that we may not use the dogmatism of unbelievers to justify our irritation and lack of patience when we hear them explain why God cannot be a valid answer for man.

Without patience we cannot be at peace because we have no right to security in our faith while so many of our fellow men stand at our door shouting that *we* are the atheists, that we are the idolaters, the lazy ones of history, the cowards, the most involved in tyranny, and that we do all this in the name of Christ the Liberator.

Today more than ever the Spirit is manifesting Himself to believers to test their faith through the mysterious, paradoxical action of atheism. I call it paradoxical because I believe that we have not yet had the courage to accept the fact that the Christian God is an unknown God who reveals Himself and appears precisely when and where we don't expect Him.

All through the centuries we have not known how to translate into our own language and apply to our own historical circumstance certain frightening statements made by Christ; for example, His telling us bluntly that sinners and prostitutes will go before us into the kingdom of heaven—a judgment that has nothing "moralistic" about it. If someone today had the courage to take our Lord's words literally, I wonder would he escape being accused of blasphemy and pelted with stones.

I think that today the only way to answer the call of God is to realize that finding Him means finding our fellow men. And finding our fellow men means finding ourselves. It is to be conscious of living—to understand that everything has a relationship to us, that everything is ours. It is to discover love, not the love of an actual encounter, but a love that urges us outwards towards everything and everybody; a love that does not just accept but that tends towards transforming all things; a love which, if it is not creative, is powerless, as Marx said; or deceptive, as St. John the Evangelist said; or damning, as Christ said.

Our search for love has so far been painful because we have not been able to transform things. Only when we succeed in doing this will our love be spontaneous, our very own, a joyful discovery and not pain or impatience.

The best way to find out if this love of ours is real is to see whether it tends towards the most refined form of egoism, love of self and of the handful of people who think as we do; or whether it tries, on the contrary, to communicate and work with all men in an effort to find in them that spark of love which no man lacks, even though he be the worst of Judases.

If our love is not motivated by and directed towards a full, loving relationship with each and every man, then it is not love at all. Our first relationship of love with all men must be to work together with them to rebuild all the structures and change all the forms of life that are contrary to this loving fellowship. Only then will it be possible to create that new man who fulfills himself by building the world along with others.

This is the aim of those who call themselves atheists, although they do not regard it as love because we have emptied this term of all meaning by confining it to the future, to heaven. Their aim is the same as ours, but they call it "justice," "liberation," or "revolution." And that is the explanation of their violence.

But what sort of purpose is this which, at one and the same time, urges the atheists towards violence and us towards unity?

Even though the means we each employ are so different, we know that we both want to attain the same end, that is, a full, human relationship with all men without special privileges and without frontiers. Experience has shown me that, in one way or another and with varying degrees of generosity, patience, originality and faith, this is the deepest need of those who are able to inquire into the reason for their lives without fear of placing their own certainties in jeopardy. Hence I ask myself if I must not regard the songs, or cries, or sighs of all my fellow men as God's voice calling me.

If I must, then I shall have to make my own the words of a modern writer (whose faith I do not know): "If we content ourselves with saying, 'I can't tell how other people feel about it, but what counts with me is my own personal experience,' then we're taking up a very puzzling position. When I'm walking along the street, I must continually feel that the people I see or meet and chat with—and such conversations almost never touch on anything connected with God—that between me and them something takes place that has God in it. If this does not happen, then one's fellow men will only be passing shadows about whom one understands nothing."

Naturally, to accept this as a real commitment, to build up this relationship with all men, believing in the richness or unique originality of each one and to do so without having ready solutions for the problems that must inevitably arise, is a real struggle, the true continual revolution, without immediate results, without mutual understanding and with the anxiety of Abraham always at our shoulder.

At such moments there is always the satanically subtle temptation to flee from the field of battle and build our own little paradise, which is not the same as God's paradise since His is for everyone. Christ did not form the first community by choosing only the elect, the pure, the aristocrats of the spirit, but by gathering in simple folk, the weak, the publicans, the prostitutes, the fishermen.

But it is not exactly a question here of "imitating" Christ, a term which I'd prefer not to use. Instead, I think that the time has come to *understand* Christ; above all, to understand that He came to reveal to us what man is and how he can realize himself fully.

We must find this secret or create it moment by moment by being faithful to our consciences, just as Christ found it by being faithful to His Father.

Christ became incarnate, became one of us, and so we can discover Him only to the extent that we discover and fulfill ourselves.

A friend of mine once wrote to me, "I believe that Christ is God because I see that He is man in every respect. Only by being God is it possible to be completely man."

Another friend, a well-known Italian Communist, wrote: "When religion strips itself of all explanations outside the truly human dimension, then there will be neither atheists nor holy Joes."

Yet these two statements may not be as different as they appear at first.

The truth is that it is not man who makes no sense without God, but rather that God would make no sense for us without man; at least, our Christian God wouldn't, since He is so irreversibly "man."

That is why I was able to state publicly to a large audience (some of whom I scandalized), "If I had to choose between God and you, I'd choose you!" The reason is simple: God Himself asked me to choose man.

If He didn't intend me to do so, then why did He tell us that at the Last Judgment He will say to those who chose Him and forgot man: "I do not know you"; while to those who chose man and ignored Him (since they did not even know about Him), He will say: "Come, you are loved by my Father!"

Truly Christianity is a scandal.

13

Searching for God Is Not Atheism

We have been taught to regard faith as something so sure and so full of certainty that the least doubt or the smallest attempt to dig deeper into it seems like a "temptation" and a sin; but true faith is really a continual search, for it is not possible to believe once and for all time. Faith is a constant growth because it is living; if it did not grow, it would be dead.

But in the history of every growth there are periods of silence, obscurity, doubt and temporary loss of one's identity. Something like this happens in our biological growth. At times, we do not know whether or not we are fully ourselves; we feel different, pulled this way and that by the continual birth and death of elements within us.

Many parents today are worried because they think their children are becoming atheists when they see them searching earnestly for a more mature faith. But the opposite is the case. Parents should be worried instead about those young people for whom everything is clear, safe and certain and who therefore feel no crisis in their faith. It is this self-assured faith that the parents should

71

be anxious about. A love that is not in ferment, that is not a torture as well as a joy, is only halfhearted. So, too, with faith.

Hence I do not regard as superficial the young people of today who are searching—quite the contrary! Not so long ago, meeting a boy or girl of eighteen who was thinking, searching and making responsible choices, and capable of directing his or her own life, was an occasion for joy and wonder. But today such young people are almost commonplace. And this often makes older folk remark, half in exasperation but also half in admiration, "At that age, we were still children, tied to the apron strings of mother and church, incapable of thinking for ourselves."

But nowadays, although the way young people think may be difficult to understand, they are showing us that they have well-defined personalities and original ideas. And this is true especially in their attitude towards the faith, the tensions they feel in it and their urge to investigate it further. Today's youth are much more mature, more thoughtful and more conscious of their belief as well as of their disbelief than perhaps young people ever have been before.

I was made especially aware of this the other day when I read out to a group of adults a short meditation which they thought was a page from the spiritual diary of some saint, whereas actually it was a prose poem written by a girl, a carpenter's daughter without much education, who was working and studying at the same time.

Certainly, those who knew this girl's love for life, the joy she radiated, the way young men flocked around her, and her apparently carefree attitude to life in general, never guessed that, beneath the girlish facade, a deep, mature, serious Christian search for truth was going on. Yet she regarded herself as an unbeliever.

She wrote:

> I'm eighteen years old, and I'm an old woman.
> I'm eighteen, and I'm tired.
> I'm eighteen, and I'm empty.

But was she really empty?

She continued:

> I don't know how to pray.
> I don't know how to love.
> I don't know how to believe.
> I don't know how to find what I'm looking for.
> Everything slips through my hands.
> When I look at something, anything, I can't see its
>   real meaning.

But can an honest searcher ever be less "empty" than when he feels he cannot reach the "real meaning" of things? Only he who is beginning to touch the infinite is capable of seeing the essential emptiness of everything finite.

In her longing for life, the girl went on:

> I'd like to be able to give;
> I'd like to be able to enjoy things;
> but, above all, I'd like to live.

To live for what? Her answer shows how mature she was:

> I don't want to waste time, Lord;
> I don't want to squander this precious gift.
> Perhaps it's my eagerness to live fully,
> my desire to find something real,
> that's urging me on.
> But, Lord,
> I'm also in a hurry to find you.

However, like so many other sincere young people today, she could not accept as her God the God that others had constructed and were seeking, nor could she adopt as her own a religious experience that she had not felt both as a joy and a torment in her own flesh:

> But, Lord, do you even exist?
> I search for you, but I can't find you.
> Where are you?

> In the sun? in the leaves of the trees?
> In me?
> In others?
> In books?
> In work?
> In love?
> I'm in a hurry to find you.
> But I'm alone,
> alone among so many people
> whom I regard as strangers, afar off.
> Yes, I'm in a hurry to find you;
> but I'm in more of a hurry to search for you.

I must confess that I feel no fear for young people such as this girl. I'm not even afraid of their atheism. Indeed, I prefer their apparently fruitless searching to the self-satisfied security of a faith that produces nothing and is never in doubt but which also has no poetry and no verve in it.

I'd like to remind this girl and others like her of the famous words of St. Augustine, "You would not be looking for me if you had not already found me," to which a modern writer has added, "... and you would never have found me if you had not gone on looking for me."

The girl's desperate plea "Where are you, Lord?" is one that is being continually made by those who are seriously seeking new roots for their faith. The most important thing is to go on searching.

But why do we even think of searching for God? Why this urge to find Him?

Is it not perhaps because He is already within us, continually arousing in our hearts a desire for communion with Him?

A Letter to Those Who Feel Insecure

Judging by the letters I receive from friends and strangers, I must conclude that insecurity is one of the characteristics of our time and that many people suffer greatly from it.

Some of them confuse insecurity with fear, perhaps because they haven't analyzed the question properly. And to these I'd like to say that insecurity and fear are two very different things. Insecurity is a lack of certainty, whereas fear is a lack of love. Fears and uncertainties are not cast out by certainties but by love.

As St. John the Evangelist tells us, "There is no fear in love, but perfect love casts out fear.... And he who fears is not perfected in love" (1 Jn 3:18). He who loves is not paralyzed by uncertainty but is capable of resolving his doubts serenely.

St. Augustine said, "In doubt, freedom," but freedom and love are intertwined. By itself, love does not bring security, but it does help us to make a firm choice. And he who acts with love loses his fear of choosing even though he may still have doubts that his choice is the best one.

Those who are perfectly secure and think they possess the whole truth may thereby be in danger of cutting themselves off from the possibility of reaching out for new horizons. They don't want to listen; they're self-sufficient; and they end up impoverished.

Those who are fearful have lost hope in themselves and in others. They can't believe in the apparently impossible, and they regard everyone as a potential enemy. Hence they always go armed, always expecting an attack, always on the defensive.

Fear is the opposite of love.

The fearful man is always afraid of losing something. But love wants to give rather than keep; and so he who loves is not afraid, because he doesn't mind giving up things.

The person who is uncertain is conscious of his own limitations and so is willing to search further. However, it would be a mistake to glorify doubt and insecurity, because the insecure man may be so lacking in the courage to choose that he is completely paralyzed. Yet it would be unrealistic to try to eliminate doubt and insecurity entirely from our lives, for this would mean losing contact with the real world, in which we are inevitably exposed to attack by uncertainties and doubts of all kinds. Here on earth, absolute and definitive truth is beyond our reach.

But it takes some depth of soul, and hence of love, to go on living in insecurity, not giving up hope, not becoming paralyzed with fear, but continuing to work at building up a provisional but nonetheless real world.

Moreover, having the courage to accept our continued uncertainty is an act of human—and divine—realism, because, as we know from the Bible, we have here no lasting city but must always go forward cautiously, perhaps having to retrace our steps again and again, and convinced that our only certainty is that we are pilgrims on earth, making our way hesitantly towards a land that no one has ever seen.

It is quite easy to understand the feelings of those who have hitherto been perfectly secure but who now see the fortifications of their certainties tumbling around their ears.

For example, take those who were sure that rigid authoritarianism and a strict hierarchy were essential to any political structure; that a religion was the only way to reach God; that possession and instinct were the only ways to true human love; and that man's real liberation came only through ideology, theology, anthropology or ecology.

But this situation does not arise for the man who knows that there are no ready-made roads but that we must make our own roads as we go; or for him who knows that we free ourselves from what is old only by accepting what is new and not by exercises in aesthetics.

Actually, Christ has not one word of reproach for those who are insecure whereas He did not spare those who felt secure; for instance, He reproved Peter for being "sure" that he would never betray Him. Yet He didn't like men to be fearful either: "Why are you afraid, O men of little faith?"; "Do not be afraid. I have overcome the world." And at the supreme moment of death, He Himself was pierced by doubt: "My God, my God, why have you forsaken me?"

Still, He was not afraid; He did not turn back but launched Himself onto the dark, yet secure, sea of love: "Father, into your hands—which I now feel as unknown, strange, disconcerting, even cruel—I commend my spirit," because I was born, lived and died, not to do My will but Yours, and You have asked Me to utter the last definitive word of love.

Even Mary, God's Mother, felt the pangs of doubt: "How can this be, since I do not know man?" And Joseph, her husband, at first doubted her enough to seriously consider putting her aside.

The disciples of John the Baptist were not sure that Jesus of Nazareth was the promised Messiah, so John sent them to ask Him point-blank: "Are you the Christ, or must we look for someone else?"

But they all made their final choice out of love.

Love means having more confidence in someone else than in oneself.

St. John the Evangelist tells us that "He who does not

love does not know God" (1 Jn 3:8) ; and in like manner, he who does not love will never have any security and will never have the courage to make a final choice.

Fear begets idleness, which is the sign of non-love, since love is impulse, movement, creativity, struggle, risk, fatigue. The day God gets tired of loving mankind, the world will become one vast, cold cemetery. Our Lord told us not to fear those who can kill our bodies but those who can kill our hope, that is, our love.

Christ never asks for absolute certainty or security; but He does ask for faith. And he who has faith is not afraid, although he may not have absolute certainty at every moment. We don't have to be able to prove the Resurrection of Christ. If only we believe, we need have no fear of not rising again, in spite of all the rationalistic objections.

But where does faith come from?

It comes from the confidence we have in the one we love.

Today people feel more need to search for love than for truth, for man than for dogmas.

When Pope John, at the end of his life, was accused of placing too much faith in men, an attitude that could be interpreted as downgrading doctrine, he replied: "The one thing I don't want to stop is loving."

In the darkness of doubt and uncertainty, it won't be the intellectuals but the wise, it won't be the theologians but the saints, who will best discern the shape of the new world that is springing up around us.

For it is new, and we need new eyes to see it.

15

The Scandal Christ Gave in Nazareth

Christ was a continuous source of scandal to his fellow townsmen of Nazareth. But there came a time when He so angered them that, as the Gospel tells us, they rushed Him out of the town and brought Him to the top of a cliff, intending to throw Him to His death.

What had He done to arouse them so much?

Nothing out of the ordinary. He had simply read a passage from Scripture and commented on it. He had spoken about freedom, but with the additional detail that the passage He had just read to them was no longer mere words but had just then become a reality.

This is how the Gospel describes the event:

> And he came to Nazareth, where he had been brought up; and he went to the synagogue, as his custom was, on the sabbath day. And he stood up to read; and there was given to him the book of the prophet Isaiah. He opened the book and found the place where it was written, "The Spirit of the Lord is upon me, because he has anointed me to preach good

news to the poor. He has sent me to proclaim release
to the captives and recovering of sight to the blind,
to set at liberty those who are oppressed, to proclaim the acceptable year of the Lord." And he closed
the book, and gave it back to the attendant, and sat
down; and the eyes of all in the synagogue were
fixed on him (Lk 4:16-20).

The audience waited with the same kind of expectant
curiosity that congregations today feel when those priests
who are reputed to be "givers of scandal" begin to comment on certain passages from the Gospel that have just
been read in the Liturgy of the Word.

In His commentary, Christ spoke one single sentence
so explosive that His hearers did not allow Him to continue but rushed Him outside to kill Him.

And what did He say that was so outrageous? Simply:
"Today this scripture has been fulfilled in your hearing."

This was the cause of the scandal, the anger, the fear
and the surprise; merely something that had hitherto
only been preached and that had therefore bothered no
one, but that now suddenly came true, became a reality.

If Christ had said: "The day will arrive when this will
come to pass," or: "We must set about putting this
prophecy into effect," or: "The poor and the oppressed
have a right to the fulfillment of this prophecy of Isaiah,"
then no one would have become angry. Who knows how
many times other rabbis and doctors of the Law had commented on these same words, expressing many pious
wishes? But the moment someone said: "*Today* these
words have come true," the world seemed to explode into
flames, at least for the men of Nazareth.

Even further, I'd say that the furor really erupted
when Christ gave concrete examples, thereby showing
that freedom would come first to strangers, to those who
did not belong to the house of Israel because they had
more faith than the Israelites, since "no prophet is acceptable in his own country" (Lk 4:24).

Christ gave two actual examples that enraged His listeners: "And he said, 'Truly I say to you, there were
many widows in Israel in the days of Elijah, when the

heaven was shut up three years and six months, when there came a great famine over all the land; and Elijah was sent to none of them but only to Zarephath, in the land of Sidon, to a woman who was a widow. And there were many lepers in Israel in the time of the prophet Elisha; and none of them was cleansed, but only Naaman the Syrian' " (Lk 4:23-27).

After that, He was unable to continue because they dragged Him outside, and He escaped death only by a miracle.

We can say that in the synagogue in Nazareth Christ introduced the "new liturgy" which replaced that of the Old Testament. In the liturgy of Christ's time, the doctors and Levites used to read a passage from the Scriptures and then comment on it, or they at least tried to arouse feelings of repentance or joy in their listeners. But the fulfillment of the Scriptures, or the prophecies, was always spoken of as taking place in an uncertain future.

Christ was the first to take the final step, bringing the future into the present and turning wishes and hopes into realities.

If this occasion was really the first liturgy of the New Testament, we must confess that today, after twenty centuries, we have to a great extent returned to the liturgy of the Old Testament, confining ourselves to merely reading the words of Scripture as if they were just pious hopes and useless promises that leave everything just as it is.

Today, too, the fulfillment of God's words is always left to the uncertain future. Our liturgies are very like the secular liturgies of the politicians, in which everything is solved in the future and never in the visible, palpable present.

Very rarely does our liturgy convey Christ's novel message at Nazareth in which, commenting on the prophecy of Isaiah foretelling liberation from all oppression and poverty, He placed His life in danger by proclaiming: "Today this scripture has been fulfilled in your hearing" (Lk 4:21). This is precisely why so many good men see the Church as just another political party and regard clerics as so many politicians who make promises they never intend to keep.

Therefore, if we are to preserve the very credibility of God's words, we must proclaim and preach them as Christ did, as an accomplished fact. "Today" is the key word for every honest man who has no desire to live on promises and hopes of a false Utopia. I remember the surprise created at a liturgical convention when, after the reading of the Gospel account of the cure of the paralytic—"Get up and walk!"—a young man of about twenty-five stood up and said, "This is what has happened to me today!" And he continued, "I came to this meeting very antagonistic to your faith, but now I accept it without reservation. I know that when I go back to the place I work in, I shall be very much alone and may even be in danger. But right now I feel only the deep joy of my election, which I want to share with everyone else." And as happened with Christ in the synagogue at Nazareth, all eyes were fixed on him, for the people of our generation need action and it is the language they understand best. Today no one believes in mere promises, whether in politics or religion.

"Witness" is perhaps one of the most overused words we hear nowadays, but in a way it is our very own word, up-to-date, for it expresses something that we need now.

To go on reading the word of God that promises freedom to the oppressed and yet to stand around with our arms folded, waiting for this freedom to drop from heaven, is to act in a way that still belongs to the liturgy of the Old Testament.

Perhaps that is why a gesture like that of Camilo Torres won the admiration of the world and even of those who did not agree with the means he used to free his people. But the course he took—turning aside from preaching the word of God and going out to fight for the liberation of his oppressed brothers—was surely a more creative and evangelical gesture than many of our liturgies in which nothing ever happens and which were a reproach and an occasion of remorse for Camilo Torres every time he celebrated the Eucharist.

To proclaim "From today on, the Church will strip herself of every institution that impedes liberation from all oppression, whether material or spiritual, of the individual or of the community," and to begin putting this proclamation into effect immediately, as Christ did, is to begin the new liturgy of the kingdom.

On the other hand, to go on reading: "Blessed are the poor.... The poor shall have the Gospel preached to them...," and then wait for these things to happen by themselves—still belongs to the old liturgy.

To announce that: "Today the Church, the Vatican, the dioceses, parishes, religious communities, Christian families and every one of the faithful have freely chosen poverty, simplicity and financial insecurity, and are going to evangelize the poor first of all" is to put into effect the liturgy of Christ and make it come true for all the world to see.

To go on reading: "My kingdom is not of this world," and then to continue weeping and sighing for a freer kingdom, but not doing anything to hasten the coming of that kingdom, is only the old liturgy once more, the liturgy of Deuteronomy.

To preach that the Church, from today on, will surrender herself totally and exclusively to the power of the Spirit, leaving aside all traces of temporal, earthly power, all human security and privilege, all political compromise, all economic worries, all wordly fears, and living joyfully in the hope of Christ, who said, "Do not be afraid. I have overcome the world," is to imitate Christ's creative gesture at Nazareth.

To go on reading and teaching that every baptized person is a priest and prophet is only the old liturgy over again.

But to preach:

that from today onward the charisms of the Church will be finally freed;

that every Christian can, as far as his conscience allows, shout aloud his own prophetic word although it may disconcert or scandalize us;

that the Church accepts every profoundly human act of the Christian as a liturgical and priestly gesture and not merely as a devotional curiosity—all his tears and his every moment of true love, all his limitations and each of his creative achievements;

that we be allowed to foster free and liberating relationships with others, without fear and without any trace of Manicheism, and by these relationships to participate in building up the final kingdom, which has already begun;

—all this so that we can say with Christ: "Today we have at least begun."

And this, this proclamation that the word of God is beginning to be a living reality must be made at each moment and at every level, from the successor of St. Peter to the humblest priest, from the pastor of each parish to the youngest of his flock capable of reading the Gospel.

Today it is not enough for the Church and each of her members to keep on saying that Christianity is freedom. We must say instead: "Today freedom has finally been allowed into, and is accepted by, the Church, with all the consequences and risks which that entails, as a ray of hope for a world that daily believes less and less in freedom. Today freedom has arrived for everyone, from the first of the faithful to the newest convert."

It is not enough to say: "St. Paul tells us that everyone is called to freedom," but rather: "From today on, you are allowed to live your Christian freedom to the full."

The claims of responsibility, the difference between liberty and license, will be sorted out later. Christ did not take away Judas' freedom but allowed him to go on to his final betrayal.

Rather than say, "Be careful," we must say, "Go ahead confidently and fearlessly!"

It is not enough to tell the members of a parish that they are responsible for the parish along with their pastor. Instead, they must be told, "From today on, you have your special part to play in everything, from balancing the budget to making the most important decisions in the parish."

It is true that, when this happens, we must be ready, as Christ was in Nazareth, to run a very serious risk to our prestige, comfort and peace of mind.

But it is also true that, while some of our liturgies could have been valid in the context of the Old Testament, today they can easily be—and often are—mere hypnotism to make us close our eyes to present reality and to the disconcerting new message that Christ has given us.

16

The Paradox of the Gospel

Some people reject the Gospel because it doesn't provide them with ready-made answers or recipes for the concrete problems of everyday life.

For example, the Gospel does not teach us what political line to follow or what party to vote for. Nor does it solve our specific moral problems for us. Thus it doesn't tell us plainly whether abortion is lawful or not, or whether we can use violence in our struggle for justice.

It does not offer us a clear course of action to follow in matters pertaining to our rights over our own bodies; for example, it does not tell us plainly whether or not we have a right to commit suicide.

However, the Christian revelation, the teachings of the Gospel, are important precisely because they don't give us concrete, permanent answers to all the possible problems that may be encountered by all men for all time. In fact, we should reject such a Gospel, because a mature person cannot accept a faith which gives him a ready answer to every problem in his life. The Gospel is only a light that continually helps us to pierce the darkness of doubt as

87

we search for answers to our individual problems. But we are the ones who have to search and find because we are free and because God has given us responsibility for fashioning our lives and our own segment of history. We are not mere enforcers of the moral law, members of a vice squad, even for ourselves, but protagonists of life, makers of history.

And this is one of the fundamental truths of the Gospel, one of the most important things Christ came to teach us. A different Gospel would be sheer fascism. Every individual has a right to search in person and in community with others.

No one can permit us, even in the name of the Gospel, to prefabricate definitive, unchangeable solutions to the problems that beset our lives and our human options. To do so would be to use the Gospel incorrectly; and it is this very misuse of the Gospel that has led many good people to reject the Christian revelation.

Revelation does not provide us with specific formulas but gives us something more important: it assures us that, since God became man without ceasing to be God, He will allow us—though we don't know exactly how—to become God without ceasing to be men. Indeed, we are already on the way to this divinization.

The responsibility of helping to carry out the task of creation and redemption can be entrusted only to a person who has been called to become Christ.

Only to such a one can be given the gift of freedom, which is an exclusive prerogative of God. Only he can be permitted to create and to work miracles. Christ has told us: "You shall do even greater things than I." Only he can be allowed to love, for love is the very life of God: "God is love" (1 Jn 4:8).

Since all this is true, since Christ came to bring us the incredible news that we have been called to do divine things, it is clear that He has not imparted to us merely a moral code, or an ideology, or a political system, or a religion, or a philosophy.

Instead, He has given us life, because He is life itself. And He hasn't given it to us in the past, but here and now, because He is not dead but living, because He never handed in His resignation and appointed a successor. He is still the center of history, the head of the Church, the heart of the world.

In short, He has given us Himself.

As for the rest, He did not bring us anything startlingly new. The things He revealed were already present in the depths of our being. They are all needs which each of us feels more or less keenly. All He did was confirm our vague yearnings or suspicions and tell us: "Yes, you're right! You won't die like an animal. In a very real sense, you are immortal. You are free; you can love; you are the kings of creation. Someone has overcome the world's fear. Happiness is possible."

It is true that to accept the Gospel we must be able to follow a line of paradoxical reasoning, since Christ was a master of paradox. We must remember that, as man, He was a native of the Middle East and not a Western European. It is useless to try to understand Him with Aristotelian logic since He was anything but a Greek.

The first paradox is revelation itself. Christ became the Word made flesh even though He knew that no human word is capable of revealing or translating God. We must grasp the idea that revelation is not a mere philosophical fact but is Christ Himself. No words, for example, can reveal to someone why I love him: I myself, in person, must reveal it to him.

Today there is more doubt than before as to whether or not it is possible to accept the idea of a transcendent God without necessarily arriving at Christ, and also as to whether or not man's present search for truth will lead him to reject both God and Christ, a doubt that arises, I believe, from the fact that man does not easily renounce being truly man, even to become God.

Man's vocation and constant yearning to become God are being challenged by his increasing need to be truly man.

Today we must find Christ revealing Himself in man, or we won't find Him at all. But does this mean that Christ is disappearing from history, or does it indicate, instead, that He is revealing Himself again?

Many people are afraid that men may fashion their

own personal Christ according to their individual specifications. However, I think the danger lies elsewhere. It is clear that every man is inclined to paint his own portrait of Christ, and I don't see how it could be otherwise. Who could hope to provide mankind with the final, definitive portrait of the infinite Son of God? Even if some genius succeeded in combining in one painting all the spiritual beauty of every saint that ever lived, the resulting portrait would not even be a shadow of the reality of Christ.

I believe, instead, that the danger lies in creating a Christ for oneself out of "anti-history." This has been the danger and the sin of the various forms of historical Christianity. And this danger is all the more grave the more we forget that the real Christ, Jesus of Nazareth, was a man of paradoxes.

Even the Apostles were incapable of creating a paradoxical Christ. In fact, they did not really understand Him until the Holy Spirit led them to accept the paradox of the Incarnation, of God becoming man.

But is Christ really paradoxical, or is it rather our "anti-historical" nonacceptance of Him that makes Him seem paradoxical to us who are steeped in "anti-history"?

Yet Christ can scarcely be anything but paradoxical since He is the only man who never accepted the contradictions of history. He is the only man who did not allow Himself to be built up from outside, who never submitted to being manipulated by others, who never allowed Himself to be judged by an external law but only by fidelity to Himself.

Therefore He is the only truly creative man, the only one who succeeded in making a segment of "real history." He is the only one who has spoken words that are true; hence He seems paradoxical to us who are only too accustomed to those that are false.

Lao Tze has said that, in paradoxical logic, "Words which are strictly true seem paradoxical." And this holds good for deeds also. In paradoxical logic, the important thing is not the words but the actions. Yet Christ did not become a thought but an "act," a reality, a man of flesh and blood.

In Western logic the opposite happens: truth is sought

in thought, and hence arise all the arguments and heresies. For us Westerners, the man who believes in God, although he does not live in Him, feels superior to those who don't believe in God, or at least say they don't, but who are really living in Him. In Christ's eyes, the good Samaritan, heretic though he was, had more faith than the priest or Levite who did nothing to help the wounded stranger by the wayside.

For us Westerners, faith equals thought, and conscience equals reason. For Christ, the Oriental, faith equals the experience of being one with God in the depths of the heart: "My Father and I are one." And conscience equals the word of God within man.

Paradoxical logic may not help us to make more scientific discoveries like the atomic bomb but it may perhaps allow us to have a better knowledge of man, who, if he is to be truly man, must be a perennial paradox by not accepting the contradiction that destroys him.

A paradoxical Christ does not fit well into a diplomatic Church or a scholastic theology, but He does help us to understand better that what matters is to be "in the world but not of it," to be really human and creative without accepting the contradiction of "anti-history," and so to be "in the structure without being in the system."

The Church of today may have lost credibility because she did not have the courage to take the risk of the Gospel paradox. In spite of Christ's being the most paradoxical of men, He was the most genuine and real human being who ever lived. He was not against authority, but He was outside it.

He was not argumentative but creative; and therefore He was necessarily a revolutionary, but without making a career of it.

He did not "conquer," because then He would have created another "order," another power. His scale of values was different from ours; the woman taken in adultery was important to Him, not because she was a sinner, but because she was a person.

He had no need of sacraments, because, since all His words were "true," they effected what they signified; or, if you prefer, in Him everything was a sacrament. The sacraments are necessary in a world in which there are no true words; or if there are such words, they are too rare.

Christ seems paradoxical to us because He created His history in a way that is the opposite to ours. He did not believe in power or arms or diplomacy: He never thought of making a concordat with Herod or Pilate. Instead, He believed in the power of the downtrodden, the strength of the weak and the violence of truth. He created His own history by sharing with others, not a prefabricated political program, but Himself.

Here are some of his more shocking "contradictions" and paradoxes.

He lived solely for His Father—the "vertical" dimension—but man was so important to Him that He did not hesitate to break the Law to cure a cripple's withered hand.

He was both God and man, yet He preached elsewhere than in the Temple, preferred mercy to sacrifice, warned His hearers not to pray like the pagans and announced that the day would arrive when men would adore God in their hearts, in justice and truth, and not necessarily in special places or buildings.

He blessed those who brought peace, and proclaimed that He had come to bring, not peace, but the sword, and to separate father and son.

He spoke in parables so that they would not understand Him.

He preached the dignity of man and respect for the humblest person on the face of the earth; but He was bitingly ironic and implacably severe with the Pharisees and contemptuous of the powerful.

He came to forgive sins, but He condemned the Pharisee who proclaimed his virtues aloud in the Temple.

He made Peter, the "apostate" Apostle, the head of His Church.

He founded a Church with power to judge and condemn, but He stressed the primacy of conscience over the law.

He opposed the doctors of the Law, but He declared that He had not come to abolish the Law but to fulfill it.

Today, however, we are beginning to discover in Christ's paradoxes the only solution to some of humanity's problems.

Hitherto it seemed impossible that Christ, true God and true man, should have had moments of doubt, disappointment, surprise, discouragement and despair; in a word, that He should have been able to taste to the full the bitterness and pain of human limitations. Nowadays we think otherwise, and from this we can take hope.

Many people believe that man cannot possibly have been called to a divine destiny. They cannot believe that he is now in a process of resurrection in the kingdom of God since there are still so many things about which he cannot be certain. But if Christ, who was both God and man, could experience fear and doubt, why shouldn't we, too, feel these emotions, we who are not yet God, although we do feel the need to be so?

It is not surprising that our certainty carries within it the sting of doubt and crisis, since this doubt and crisis are part and parcel of the basic poverty of man, who has not yet realized himself fully, for he is still a citizen of time.

That is why our salvation is never assured but is still an adventure, a battle unwon.

17

A Letter to Good People

Who are the good people of this world?

A workman once said to me, "We are all worse than we think we are but better than other people's opinion of us."

Few of us complacently assent when others say we are "good," yet few of us think we're bad, and we would object strongly if anyone suggested we were. I believe there are no completely good people because no one in the world is so lily-white in every respect that he can afford to cast the first stone at any sinner. However, we can say that some people are less bad than others, because love is not entirely dead in the world.

There are some who live off others, and there are some who willingly die for their fellowmen. There are those who can sincerely rejoice in their neighbor's good fortune, and others who are consumed with envy of the smallest happiness that comes their brother's way. There are wolves and there are sheep; there is honey and there is gall. Hatred, revenge and the black market exist, but so do generosity, pardon and unselfishness.

There are flower gardens, and there are garbage dumps.

There is good wheat, and there are weeds.

But Christ did not want the weeds plucked from the wheat field, which perhaps means that it is not easy for us to distinguish between them.

Hence it is not easy to write to the good people of the world.

So I'd prefer to write to those of you who say or feel that you are good;

to those of you who too easily judge that other people are bad;

to those of you who think you're good simply because you are incapable of hating others and not because you love them;

to those of you who think you're good because you've made no mistakes, for the simple reason that you've never had the courage to take a risk for anybody or anything;

to those of you who think you're good merely because you adore a dead God who doesn't disturb you and not because you pray;

to those of you who think you're good just because you don't bother to look and see if anyone around you is weeping or in despair or can't see why he should go on living, and not because you do things for others;

to those of you who think you're good only because you regard yourselves as the faithful guardians of the past, and not because you make life a little better for others or contribute to your fellowmen's growth or progress;

to those of you who think you're good for no other reason than that you think everyone else is worse than you.

We all fall into those temptations until harsh experience teaches us:

that formidable things can sprout and grow out of weakness, wretchedness and utter ruin;

that those who pray least are often the ones who have most respect for the freedom of others;

that those who have misused human love are sometimes the most capable of responding to a sincere act of kindness;

that those who have lost all human dignity crawling through the sewers of life are not for that reason the least sensitive to the words of Christ, who came to seek and to save, not the just, but sinners;

that those who steal are not always the least generous, or those who kill, the least sensitive to the value of life.

These may seem like mere literary paradoxes, used for effect. But they're not. They're harsh realities which only life itself can teach us.

I must confess to you good people that I feel afraid when I hear a man, a family, an institution, a party or a church declaring righteously, like the Pharisee in the parable: "God, I thank thee that I am not like other men, extortioners, unjust, adulterers, or even like this tax collector" (Lk 18:11).

I am afraid, because Christ said that, of the two, it was the publican, acknowledging he was a wretched sinner, who was the good man: "I tell you, this man went down to his house justified rather than the other."

Today in our churches, communities and political parties, the Pharisee of the parable is still very much alive.

And so we must ask ourselves some searching questions. Who are the really good people? Those who have the effrontery to think privately and even declare publicly that they are good? Or those who have the courage to admit their uncertainties or their sins?

Is the Church good when she says: "We are not like other churches, because we believe in God, we defend freedom and justice and are the faithful guardians of dogma and morality"? Or when she confesses her sins—her betrayals, oppressions and scandals, present as well as past?

Is a political party good when it declares: "We are not like other parties, because we are democratic; we defend the rights of the people; we guarantee the rule of law and the freedom of our citizens"? Or when it does not promise more than it can hope to deliver; when it admits that it must struggle constantly so as not to become too corrupt; when it sincerely believes that power is evil if it does not belong to everyone; and when it confesses that it is difficult to remain honest when thievery and deception are regarded as necessary or even virtuous?

Is a religious or social group good when it says: "We are not like the others. We don't accept any firm commitments to anything, either to an authority or a structure or obedience to bosses of any kind. Instead, we reject the past and live in true communion with each other"? Or when it has the sincerity to confess that it really doesn't know for sure where it is going, or where commitment begins or ends; and when it does not know whether its efforts are revolutionary or merely reformist, and whether its love for men is Christianity or mere ideology?

Is the self-sufficient man good? Or rather the one who feels the need to share with everyone and exclude no one from his own little piece of truth and the riches of his human poverty?

It would certainly be ingenuous to think it's easy to divide the world into "the good guys" and "the bad guys," and that those people are good who regard everyone else as bad and who always think and say that they are not like the rest of men.

What we do know is that the greatest saints were those who had the greatest sins to repent.

We know, too, that the Church has not yet had the courage to meditate deeply on Christ's words to Simon the Pharisee about Mary Magdalen: "He who is forgiven little, loves little" (Lk 7:47).

In my opinion, Christ here meant that those who refuse to love because they are afraid of running any risk will certainly not be the best teachers of love.

Feeling and saying that we, individually or collectively, are good is wanting to be purer than Christ Himself, who was perturbed when someone called Him "good": "Why do you call me 'good'? One there is who is good" (see Mt 19:17).

If Christ was afraid that people would say that He was good, how is it possible that we Christians don't feel ridiculous, not merely when we think we're good and better than anyone else, but also when we become insulted and annoyed if others don't share this opinion of us?

It is certain that men are thirsting for real goodness. Hence, as happened with Christ, they are inclined to give the title "good" to almost any decent, law-abiding citizen or even to any well-conducted child. But it is always unpardonable for us to set ourselves up as models of goodness for everyone else to admire and imitate.

18

The Violent Peace of Christ

A "violent peace" is not the same as a "peaceful violence."

If I say, "Violence, yes, but . . .", I'm in danger of denying the violent strength of the Gospel.

Hence I prefer to say, "Peace, yes, but . . .", because peace is a fundamental human value; but a peace which does not have the impetus, courage and force of a true revolution is not a real peace at all.

The violent peace of Christ is very different from the peace that is presented by many of those in politics and religion and by many men in the street who are tired of fighting.

Christ Himself said, "My peace I give to you; not as the world gives do I give to you" (Jn 14:27).

But how is the peace of Christ different?

Our Lord was certainly speaking about a peace that is quite different from the one we're looking for when we plead, "Leave me alone and let me live in peace!"; and His peace is also basically distinct from the peace we're looking for when we say, "I want to live at peace with my conscience."

99

We could conclude that, for Christ, peace is equal to violence since He told us, "I have not come to bring peace but the sword." If the peace of Christ does not imply a certain violence, then I don't know what those words of His mean. And we certainly can't put them aside, as if He never said them.

If "living in peace" means being "left alone," then I cannot understand those other words of Christ either: "The kingdom of heaven has suffered violence, and men of violence take it by force" (Mt 11:12). But the kingdom of heaven is peace, because peace is man's supreme value.

How can it be that only the violent know what peace is and that only they have a right to possess it? The fact is that Christ came to bring a peace that must include the struggle against all forms of injustice and oppression. It is a peace that must be fought for and won before it can be savored. If the peace proclaimed by Christ is not in harmony with justice, then it is a peace that has nothing to say to those who are committed to building up a freer and more human world.

Unlike some Christians and some self-styled Christian governments, Christ would never have agreed with Goethe's unworthy sentiment: "I prefer injustice to disorder."

I am convinced that He would say precisely the contrary today: "Let disorder come if it must, but let justice prevail," even though disorder is inconvenient and disrupts the peaceful life of the privileged and the comfortable middle-classes.

I have always found the Gospel incident at Gadara very significant. You remember the story (Mt 8:28-34; Mk 5:1-20; Lk 8:26-39). Christ cured a possessed man by casting out the devils and sending them into a herd of swine which then rushed down into a lake and were drowned. When the people of the town saw this, they entreated Christ to go away. Why? Apparently because He had freed the possessed man. But freedom can cause fear and always has a price. The people of Gadara had to pay for having their fellow townsman freed from the power of the devils; and they thought the price, a herd of swine, too high.

There are still many of us who prefer to go on living peacefully with our swine, our comfortable self-indulgence, rather than gain a freedom that must be paid for by sacrificing our easy life or giving up some of our privileges.

Moreover, we want to have nothing to do with any prophet who proposes a costly freedom, because we have not yet understood that our own true peace begins only when our brother's peace begins and not when it ends, and that it really is not possible to be at peace while even one of our fellowmen is suffering the horrors of a satanic violence.

Christ preached a violence that brought peace, not by force of arms—He reprimanded Peter for trying to defend Him by the sword—but by the power of word and example; and at the end of all, He preferred to allow Himself to be killed rather than kill to save His life. But His peace is none the less revolutionary for that.

When John the Baptist, that violent prophet, was in prison and under threat of death from Herod, Jesus told John's disciples to go back and report to their master His liberating, revolutionary program of teaching and healing. There is no peace apart from such a liberation from oppression, physical or mental. Hence the Church has no right to speak of peace if she does not, at the same time, let everyone see plainly that she is fighting against every form of oppression and enslavement.

We continue to be scandalized by words like "struggle," "revolution," and "violence" while we take no exception to a word like "crusade," which implies violence that is used, not to free others, but to subject those who think differently from us.

Therefore, if peace cannot be separated from justice, then unbridled capitalism is war.

If peace cannot be attained without freedom, then all totalitarianism is war.

If peace cannot be won without speaking the truth aloud fearlessly, then all the Church's diplomacy is war.

If peace cannot be shaped without freedom of conscience, then all narrow-minded dogmatism and legalistic censure is war.

If Christ created peace by preaching the Gospel to the

poor, to the least of men, then we are waging war when we defend the rich and powerful.

If He came to call, not the just, the believers, but sinners, the atheists, then we are preparing for war when we ignore those who don't believe, and we are just wasting time when we lavish care on the one faithful sheep who has remained in the fold, while we know perfectly well that there are ninety-nine others wandering around lost outside. In contrast, Christ preferred to leave the ninety-nine faithful souls and go in search of the one sheep that was lost and uncertain where to turn.

The peace of Christ is not bought with money in churches, nor is it found in the sleepy corners of sacristies. Peace is costly and is a daily task. Moreover, it is a community, not an individual, effort.

Peace is the most sacred of words because it is synonymous with happiness; it is man's total happiness; in a sense, it is God Himself. And this is the very reason why it must not be invoked in vain; as the Bible puts it: "Because they have misled my people, saying: 'Peace,' when there is no peace," they will be destroyed (see Ez 13:10).

Here it is a question of the very serious temptation to deceive the people by trying to convince them that they already have peace whereas they are really living in fear and anxiety. "Order" is not the same as peace; and it is the people themselves, not their government, who must judge whether or not that government has given them real peace. Peace is not the same as resentful or fear-inspired silence.

Happily, today a new conscience has arisen in those involved in the lives of their fellowmen who are so oppressed that they haven't got even a little time to savor this silent peace. It is not enough to say, "I can sleep in peace because I have done no harm to anyone," for such an attitude is neither Christian nor human. The man who really believes in his fellowmen prefers to say: "I can't sleep in peace, because I haven't tried to help others to do so." And I have heard this said more often by nonbelievers than by those who possess a tranquil faith.

Yet it is only too easy to look for peace in silence even when we are aware that:

there are many mothers so blinded by the desperation or the neurosis which tyranny and misery produce that they kill their children;

many families are breaking up because the parents cannot communicate with each other;

many priests are leaving the priesthood because they no longer believe in a Church which they accuse of being bureaucratic and class-conscious;

many honest workers become Communists because they are disillusioned with the failures of democracy;

many young people commit suicide because their elders have robbed them of all hope of finding a meaning for their lives;

many others seek in drugs and sex what religion has not been able to give them;

many women in some parts of the world are spending money on slimming while their sisters in other places can't get enough food to keep their children alive.

True peace of conscience means being aware of these harsh realities and doing something to find solutions to them. But this necessarily means that Christian peace must be discomfiting, scandalous and violent.

The man who is violent yet peace-loving will necessarily remain just an intellectual; and the one who is peace-loving yet revolutionary will always be a martyr who, though he may not kill anyone, will himself be killed or persecuted in the name of peace, not the peace of Christ, but that of the established order, a peace which always works in favor of those in power. Christian peace will never be achieved while Christians retain their nostalgia for order and private property.

Peace is created by the capacity of some to listen to others; and perhaps it is lack of this capacity for dialogue with nonbelievers that has distorted our idea of peace. If we had had the courage to listen to those whose notion of peace is different from ours, we would have a clearer, stronger, more realistic and more human concept of peace.

Even among the most dedicated revolutionaries, it is difficult to find anyone who carries his revolution to the extreme consequences of commitment, risk and generosity. As I see it, Christ's revolution was total and all-embracing, and so it was regarded simply as political violence, although it was much more than that.

A revolution that confines itself to one dimension only is always in danger of becoming a tyranny of conformism. If we bring about a revolution solely on the political level, it may become fascism. If we do so only on the cultural level, it may turn into an ideology without any bread-and-butter benefits. If we do so merely on the economic level, it may end up as crass materialism. And if we have a revolution simply on the moral level, it may deteriorate into a sheer evasion.

If a revolution to attain peace is to be effective, it must be brought about on all levels at the same time, because man's liberation must either be total or it will be nothing more than outward conformity.

The French Marxist Roger Garaudy has pointed out that the greatest revolution in history can be found only in the Gospel—the revolution which Christ brought in the name of love. Actually, love is stronger than justice as a revolutionary force. The struggle for justice is necessary, but it is comparatively minor, since it means accepting the logic of the existing system. A revolution inspired by love goes beyond the struggle for justice because it seeks a radical change in the course of history: it is looking for a totally different world, in which, for example, trade unions will not be needed because the workers will never have to defend themselves against the bosses, for bosses will no longer exist in a community that shares everything, past and future.

The Prayer of Those Who Have No Peace

Lord,
>   we are the sorry procession of all those who have no
>   peace,
>   the ones who have been pushed aside and excluded
>   from life.
>   We are that unhappy band, the sweepings of the
>   earth—
>   the desperate,
>   the illiterate,

    the lonely,
    the displaced,
    the tormented,
    the excommunicated,
    the abnormal,
    the attempted suicides.

Among us, too, are the despised, those who are not even mentioned on the list of the works of mercy.

More often than not, despair is the only crust we have to chew on.

What can we say when we pray to you, the God of freedom and the Brother of the oppressed?

It's not easy for us even to believe in you when there are so many people who say they love you and who preach your peace to us, yet who then either exploit us shamelessly or are in an unseemly hurry to forget we exist.

When we do find someone who is not ashamed to share our struggles and our defeats, who sacrifices his own peace to win peace for us, you must forgive us if we mistake him for you and adore him as our god.

Help us at least to believe that our very wretchedness and poverty can be the source of power and peace for us, since it may perhaps be true that no one is stronger and more free than he who has nothing to lose. And who has less to lose than we?

Remind each of us in our personal deserts of solitude and loneliness that peace is not always won by force of arms and that oppression and bondage can be the seedbeds of peace and freedom.

19

The Most Dangerous Things

Which is more dangerous, freedom or tyranny? Words or weapons? Love or hate? Poverty or riches? A child or an intellectual? A friend or an enemy? Conscience or the law?

Freedom is more dangerous than tyranny because we were created for freedom. Hence, in the ashes of even the most repressive slavery, there are always a few embers of freedom left glowing, ready to burst into a flame that will devour tyranny. If tyranny is to succeed, it must smother the last sparks of freedom in men's hearts. But that would be like trying to quench the sun. Tyranny may hold entire nations in bondage, but it is already defeated because it is not natural to those who suffer under it or even to those who, though they profit by it, still do not like it. Men love freedom. One poor man who is free is more dangerous than a thousand rich slaves.

Words are more dangerous than weapons because weapons can kill only the body, whereas words can change men's lives. Weapons can conquer, but words can convince. Weapons can kill, but words can give life.

Love is more dangerous than hate because hate, like plastic, is dead and cold and incapable of striking a spark of life. But love is life and can become a flame of fire. It can do great harm; hence it carries within it the obligation to do good. No one need ever hate; but everyone must love.

Poverty is more dangerous than riches because wealth always has a limit beyond which lies disgust or neurosis. But poverty has an infinite thirst for mystery and is an open door thereto. Wealth lulls us to sleep. Poverty wakes us up. Since we have nothing to lose, it urges us on to adventure, search and risk, to crime or sanctity. Wealth isolates us and allows us to be individualists. Poverty forces us into communion with our fellowmen. It urges us to meet others, and this meeting is the most dangerous thing of all since it is the most creative and compromising.

A child is more dangerous than an intellectual. It is possible to fight an intellectual or ignore him. We can accept his ideas or reject them. But it is impossible to get away from a child. He is always there, reminding us that a life is worth more than an idea, that we are most powerful when we are defenseless and that we are loved only when we give no cause for fear.

A friend is more dangerous than an enemy. We can defend ourselves from an enemy; we can close the door on him. But we cannot defend ourselves from a friend; our door is always open to him. We can love our enemies, but we have to allow ourselves to be loved by our friends, and this is more difficult and risky. We can give our enemies what we have, but we have to give our friends even what we don't have. If our enemies forget us, we find it easy to return the compliment. But if our friends betray us, we won't be able to sleep for thinking about it.

Conscience is more dangerous than the law. The law can be changed, but conscience is eternal. The law can be discussed or even attacked, but conscience is more certain, more assured than we ourselves are.

We usually judge how dangerous a thing is by the damage it can do us. But this is not really an accurate yardstick. We are more afraid of good than of evil. Hence good is more dangerous than evil. We can reject evil and remain at peace with ourselves. But if we reject what is good, we become prey to constant remorse.

The fact that we cannot defend ourselves against good as well as we can against evil is the best proof that good, and not evil, is connatural to us.

20

A Letter to the Pharisees

The Pharisees are those who are devoted to immobility.
They are the bitterest and most secret enemies of all that
is new. And they are very much alive today. They continue to exist in all the churches, synagogues and other institutions. They are not a relic of the times of our Lord
but are as active now as they were then.

They were the powerful legalistic and formalistic element in ancient Judaism and were execrated by Christ,
who called them anything but soft names—"whited sep-
ulchres," "brood of vipers," "blind guides." And today,
by universal consent, they are being called even harsher
things.

The Pharisees of today, like their counterparts of old,
deceive, terrorize and use the simple and the ignorant
in the name of a law, a system of order, a set of supposed-
ly sacred values, which are really only devices to protect
or promote their own self-interest or comfort. But fortunately people are beginning to see through these schemes.

If the Church had always had the courage to judge
morality, not by the standards of Manichean theologies

or philosophies, but in the light of Christ's reactions to men's actual attitudes, we would not now find ourselves with a world conscience that is smothered and almost incapable of discovering the real evil, the real sin, the real apostasy.

The day is not yet past when clerics and zealous laymen launch anathemas from pulpits, platforms and newspapers against certain "scandals" but say nothing to the Pharisees inside and outside the Church and even make concordats with them and join with them in organizing crusades against immorality of the flesh while they keep silent about immorality of the spirit.

Christ never condemned those weaknesses which we preach against so frequently. But He did denounce certain sins that we have come to accept and, in some cases, even approve. He never said: "Woe to you who rebel in order to get justice! Woe to you, adulterers! Woe to you who do not keep the Sabbath! Woe to you, atheists! Woe to you, young agitators!" Nor did He ever condemn any man for a personal weakness.

But He did condemn those who take away other people's right to live, those who prevent others from finding out the truth, from living in freedom and from fighting for what they believe.

Hence He condemned those who try to lord it over others; those who, in the name of God, impose on others their own idea of truth, their own law, their own morality, their own culture, their own political party, smothering the creative freedom of the sons of God: "Woe to you, scribes and Pharisees, hypocrites! because you shut the kingdom of heaven against men; for you neither enter yourselves, nor allow those who would enter to go in. Woe to you, scribes and Pharisees, hypocrites! for you traverse sea and land to make a single proselyte, and when he becomes a proselyte, you make him twice as much a child of hell as yourselves. Woe to you, blind guides... (You) have neglected the weightier matters of the law, justice and mercy and faith" (Mt 23:13-16, 23).

There is, perhaps, in the Gospel no more terrible expression than the one our Lord used after curing the man born blind: "For judgment I came into this world, that those who do not see may see, and that those who see may become blind" (Jn 9:39).

When they heard this, the Pharisees, with hypocritical logic, challenged Him: "Are we also blind?" To which He replied: "If you were blind, you would have no guilt; but now that you say, 'We see,' your guilt remains" (Jn 9:40-41).

This a direct condemnation of self-sufficiency, dogmatism, puritanism, legalism and self-righteous orthodoxy.

The Pharisees were convinced that they had the most perfect knowledge of the truth and that they were the most faithful guardians of religion, even to the extent of keeping themselves aloof from sinners for fear of being contaminated by them. But Christ declared that it was they who were really blind, really the men of sin, whereas the victims of their pride and egoism were in fact those whose eyes were open and whose hearts were pure.

Now, as then, it is not the elite, the specialists, the experts, who are the true prophets of history but rather those who are so discerning that they are not frightened when they come upon a mystery; those who are able to recognize the genuineness of things and the justice of men and who are not afraid to acknowledge that they themselves are weak and fragile; those who fear that God's gift of life will go unrecognized; those who greet with joy the first gleam of light; those who don't fear that God can be offended or who aren't preoccupied with defending His Church, since their faith is real and they know that He does not need our defense but only our gratitude and love.

Only they are capable of recognizing the sincerity and genuineness of a just man. And they, along with Christ, are the severest judges of those who claim to be enlightened but who are really blind guides.

As Pope John XXIII lay dying, a well-known ecclesiastic and member of the Roman Curia who is now a Cardinal made the following astonishing announcement to the people of God who were gathered in the square of St. Peter's, praying and weeping for their dying friend and Pontiff: "Because God couldn't open his eyes, He has finally decided to close them." I wish this story had been made up, but unfortunately it is true. It is impossible to regard this incident as anything other than a revival of the most hateful pharisaism. According to this ecclesiastic, Pope John was a blind man whom God had to remove quickly so that the faithful would not be deprived of light. And, naturally, he regarded himself as a prophet who had seen that the Pope was a poor, ignorant blind man.

Yet, while he felt justified in pronouncing his condemnation on Pope John, the whole world was weeping, praying and suffering because the Pope's life was ebbing away, a life that had given a moment of hope to everyone, wise and ignorant, black and white, atheist and believer.

And Christ Himself said that it is the poor, the simple, the least of all, the victims of pharisaism and power, who will be the real judges of our success or failure as men and as sons of God.

21
"The Word of God Is Not Fettered"

A reporter arriving for a press conference was stopped at the door by police and asked what he had in his briefcase. He replied, "The most powerful bomb in the world." It turned out to be the Bible.

Perhaps because the Bible is so explosive, those in power have always tried to monopolize it. Hence using the Bible has often been taboo, almost sinful, especially for ill-instructed Catholics.

But things are changing today, and the layman's fear of the Bible is beginning to recede, so that now more than ever before the words of St. Paul are proving true: "The word of God is not fettered" (2 Tm 2:9).

Today it can be said that most of the official and spontaneous groups of believers, especially among the young, use the Bible as their main subject for meditation.

But we cannot forget that we are like a young man leaving home for the first time with all his savings to make his own way in the world and try out his wings. We are so used to having the word of God monopolized by those in power that we are still not quite able to regard it as "ours" and to believe that it really is not "fettered." And since those in power are afraid that the Bible may be used against them, they are able to find endless excuses for restricting its application.

The new insight we have gained by our discovery of the Bible helps us to see that the word of God has an explosive power that we did not even imagine before. And this is not because the Bible texts are magical words, but because they are true and because they reveal to us our inmost identity. We cannot remain neutral towards them but must be for or against them.

The words of the Bible are inexhaustible words because God goes on pronouncing them with new meaning exactly suited to each man and to each new set of circumstances. But very clearly defined conditions are needed if the word of God is to exert its full power, and, judging by the experiences of various communities, the texts of the Bible can be seen as bearers of God's word only to the extent that they fulfill these conditions:

1. Those who hear or read the Bible text must understand the terms used. It may be hard to believe, but I am continually meeting people who don't really know, for example, what a "Levite" or a "Samaritan" was in the time of Christ. Hence they are almost shocked when I explain to them that, in modern terms, a Levite could be compared to a Catholic involved in Catholic action, and the Samaritan to an atheist or an anarchist.

Many think that it was the other way around, that the Levite was the atheist and the Samaritan was the God-fearing man. Thus when I had explained the parable to a teacher friend of mine, he remarked, "We've always been told that this is the parable of the *good* Samaritan. And now you make him out to be an atheist!" Obviously, when the word of God is misunderstood in this way, it cannot be a force for revolution and conversion.

2. The text proposed to the congregation for reflection should not be completely outside their interests or their real, pressing problems. Thus scripture passages extolling the freedom of the sons of God or the joys of married life would have little relevance for the congregation in a prison.

3. The listener should really be seeking the truth; he should not be afraid of being converted or judged by the words of Scripture; and he should be able to accept the Bible texts as applicable to himself and not just to others. If these conditions are not met, even the clearest and most vivid scriptural passages will not raise a ripple in his soul.

This was the case with a certain industrialist whom I knew. He returned home from Mass one Sunday with his wife and children to find the front of his house decked out with placards bearing quotations from the Bible prophets. The signs had been prepared by some of the industrialist's Christian workers, and the quotations were very apt since they were, in fact, an examination of conscience on his selfish, authoritarian attitude towards his employees. In a perfect fury of indignation, he pulled down the placards, tore them up as if they were obscene and shouted: "This is intolerable!" He had heard the same words of Scripture used in church on many occasions, perhaps even that very Sunday morning, but then they were not "intolerable" because he had regarded them as being applicable only to others and not to him. But the placards were obviously meant only for him, and so they had struck home.

It's true that indignation is not conversion, but it's likely that when the industrialist was confronted with the plain word of God aimed at him alone, he felt it much more keenly than the same word proclaimed in church to the whole congregation and perhaps "sweetened" or watered down by the preacher.

4. The words of the Scriptures must not only be read but must also be interpreted by the whole assembly, not argumentatively but creatively, with both a penitential and a paschal spirit; and they must be interpreted by everyone, from the youngest to the oldest, from the most learned to the most illiterate.

There is much talk nowadays about a "new word" in a "new liturgy." But this is not just a question of better translations or more modern versions of the texts. These are necessary, but they are not enough. The truly new word is that which must be pronounced by those whom I would call "the silent ones," that is, those who have always had to accept the words of others without ever being able to offer their own. As long as we do not hear from the silent mass of the people of God, we shall not have the new word and, therefore, we shall lack the truly new liturgy. Everything else is mere playing at reform. We must realize that God has written His words in the hearts of all men and not just in those of a privileged few.

We ourselves cannot create a new word but must discover the unspoken words which we carry within us and which have been smothered by the schemes, fears, chains and bonds imposed on us by the various forms of tyranny that have stealthily turned to their own advantage, not only the very idea of God, but also His revealed word. In my opinion, this is the only real "desacralization" of the words of Scripture.

The words that we have in the Bible are the wrappings in which God's message has come down to us. The message is true and authentic, but the wrappings were made by men according to their culture, their own particular problems and the language of their day.

If we take the words of Scripture in their absolute sense and regard them as sacred, untouchable and untranslatable into a form that suits our modern mentality and the problems of today, then there is nothing more to be said and there can be no question of any growth in creativity, in faith and in the knowledge of the living God. This is what happened with the ancient, unchanging religions of mystery.

But if we really believe that the God of the Bible continues to pronounce His own words through the mouths of men and that He translates them every time a man discovers and applies them to his own historical needs, then those ancient words are changed into a new, creative and, in the best sense, explosive reality. But this is precisely why we are afraid to "unfetter" the word of God, to set it free and give it to those who have hitherto been silent.

There is no use in my reading God's word to a congregation if I cannot tell them what it means to me and how I interpret it in terms of my own life. At such a moment, my interpretation of the text, my translating it into faith and spirit, can become more important and more effective than the actual words of the Bible itself.

I have been present at liturgies celebrated in great freedom, where the word of God circulated "unfettered," and where truly new things have occurred. I recall one in particular. The Gospel parable of the vine and the branches had been read, and everyone freely gave a commentary on it. Finally, a gentleman in the congregation rose and said, "I am just a mailman, and it was only by chance that I came to this Mass. I didn't want to speak because I'm not an educated man. But I was never at a Mass like this before; I like it, and for the first time I feel united with everyone in the congregation. I am not as learned as the rest of you, but if you will take me as I am, I shall come back again. When I think about what Christ says in the Gospel of the Mass today, I believe that even I can be of use to you. Even though there may be a sour grape like me in the bunch, no one notices it when all the grapes are crushed. So I won't feel out of place but shall be just like the rest of you."

When the time for Communion came, the mailman, heartened by the effort he had made to speak for the first time in church and by the silent respect with which he had been heard, went over to a group of university students and shook hands with them, a thing he would never have normally done. Then a young engaged couple stood up and said, "We came here just to see what was going on. We haven't been to the sacraments for several years, but after listening to the mailman speaking, we feel we must go to Communion so as to be more closely united with him in God. This will really be our *first* Communion."

The word of God translated by the uneducated mailman was creative for the engaged couple, and if he had not spoken, nothing new would have happened for them.

At a recent liturgical celebration, one of the participants, a stranger, stood up and spoke about the Gospel reading, which had been the parable of the talents. He wanted to know why the parable didn't mention a very important character, the man who had done his best to use the talents given him but who had lost them all in the attempt. This started the group on an interesting dis-

cussion from which they concluded that such a character
did not appear because Christ did not condemn him and
hence that the Christian may risk all for God since, according to the Gospel, it is not he who loses who is condemned
but only he who does not have the courage to take a risk.
We have always esteemed prudence too highly and therefore we have been in danger of presenting as a model the
very type of person whom Christ condemned, the man who
hides the talents he received for fear of losing them. And
we have left in the shadows the very character who, as an
atheistic psychologist has said, "is really portrayed in the
parable, but whom we don't want to see, namely, Christ
Himself."

5. The words of the Bible must not be manipulated by
anyone, because they thus lose all their power, and God
continues to be invisible and incommunicable.

I remember how ill-at-ease the people of a middle-class
parish felt when their parish priest went out of his way
to give a mild interpretation of Gospel texts condemning
the rich and to speak about their "prophetic" role. This,
of course, was a complete misuse of the Bible.

If these five conditions are not fulfilled, then the words
of the Bible will not be received as containing a new message. They are not magical words but words of life, and
this life needs man and his cooperation if it is to take
flesh. Otherwise, as so often happens, the Bible will be
on the same level as the life of a saint or any other pious
book. And perhaps it won't even be that since many biblical texts are quite difficult to understand.

Consequently, if the Bible seems to have lost its relevance for many people, so that they go searching for new,
prophetic words in its stead, we are to blame: first, because we have regarded the Bible as a goal and not as a
starting point; secondly, because we have believed that
the Scriptures had exhausted the wells of prophecy, as if
God had no more to say or was no longer capable of communicating with all men of good will; and thirdly, because
we have not had the courage to present the *complete* Bible
but only the less disturbing parts.

I must admit that I was quite angry with myself when,
as I was looking at the slogans on banners and placards

prepared for a Communist rally, a militant leftist said to me, "That's the way to talk to the people and not in your empty words!" I was tempted to write under each slogan a verse from Christ or the prophets since their words were even more revolutionary than those of Marx or Lenin. And I was angry with myself because the militant leftist had once been a Catholic and so must have heard the word of God preached often but incompletely or in a mystifying way since he sincerely believed that it was "empty."

I could not fail to see the word of God in those slogans because they were merely divine revelation translated into our everyday language and expressing our current needs.

22

Suicide: the Ultimate Gesture
of Despair

Tolstoy said that all happy people are very much alike, whereas each unhappy person suffers in his own special way. If this is true, then the most individualistic and uncommon pain is that felt by those who plumb the depths of despair and commit suicide.

The suicide gives up all hope. But he also gives us cause to question our ability to love, and he passes judgment on the fragility of our hope, for we have not been able to give him any real reason to go on living. Even in our paganized modern society suicide is still the great taboo, perhaps because it forces us to do something we hate to do —examine our conscience.

The almost daily increase in the number of suicides means that there is a corresponding increase in the number of those who, because of fear of one kind or another, are unable to build up a world for themselves in which life is worth living and loving. Suicides are on the increase because our freedoms are decreasing; because our creativity is being thwarted and our consciences are being

123

shackled.

It has been estimated that a thousand people commit suicide every day and that ten thousand others attempt it. And ninety percent of those who kill themselves or try to do so were driven to it because they were unable to create something personal, something original, something of their own; because they felt they were not believed or accepted by a world that always viewed them with hostility.

It is not that anyone loves death. Indeed, a large number of those who commit or attempt suicide do it for the paradoxical reason that they are trying to find in death a meaning which they were unable to find in life. Those who cannot discover any creative values in life are almost inevitably drawn to look for the ultimate affirmation of self in the absurdity of death.

But man instinctively feels that taking one's own life is wrong, and perhaps that is why he tries to hide that most intimate and shameful wound of all, the self-administered deathblow. In every type of society, it is quite difficult to ascertain the real statistics of suicide, a fact which gives rise to several questions.

Is this universal desire to conceal self-destruction the result of religious taboos which label everyone who commits suicide as a certain candidate for Hell? Or is it caused by men's inborn horror at what has been called "the ultimate insanity"? Or does another man's suicide reproach each one of us with the fact that we were unable to make life bearable for him?

I remember when we were children that our parents forbade us to drink from a certain well because a man had drunk from it a short while before hanging himself. Even today, having a suicide in the family is regarded as a greater disgrace than having an unmarried mother, an alcoholic, a drug addict, a thief or a homosexual among one's relatives. But the fact that seventy percent of suicides are young people suggests that suicide is not so much a matter of disgrace or dishonor as of a real sickness in society caused, not by a virus, but by our lack of love for life.

If every forward step in history, every seed of humanity, must be paid for in suffering, then perhaps the deaths of those thousands of young people who freely choose to die by their own hands is the price we must pay for the knowledge that there is something profoundly wrong with our society, that the moment may have arrived for us to look into our hearts and ask whether these young people may not be right when they tell us that this world is too ugly to live in and that it must be changed radically.

Those who are responsible for society as it is today cannot regard as a merely emotional incident the suicide of the Italian girl who, just before she threw herself to her death shouted to her mother, "What are we doing in this ugly world? Come on, throw yourself out the window with me!" And how eloquent in this sense was the suicide of the young French students who set fire to themselves in a factory yard, leaving behind them a note which read: "We're killing ourselves because of the wars and insanities of mankind."

Every time a young person, anywhere in the world, puts a bullet in his head, opens his veins, takes poison or sets himself on fire, the experts in human behavior try to find the basic reasons for such madness. And they come up with all the usual answers—sexual frustration, family pressures, worry about exams, loneliness, religious crisis, rejection by society, etc. But the true reason most often remains hidden, for it is a reason that cannot be reached on the merely sociological level and is one that is addressed to both young and old, guilty and innocent.

As the German theologian, Klaus Demmer has said: "A young person who is not accepted by his family or society, who is not loved or understood, lacks the natural basis for being able to understand what it means to be loved by God with a selfless love that never betrays. He who has never really been loved by anyone can never understand what love is. And how many young people are there today who have had a serious experience of selfless love?"

A modern author, Sergio Zavoli, believes that suicides are increasing "because man has ceased to ask himself what he is and why he is alive in an era which obliges him to be what he isn't. He has ceased to ask himself this question because the meaning of our history is sometimes badly understood and because 'Thank God, it's Friday!' is a surrender and not the signal for a renewal of energy. For he can find no one who is able to proclaim without malice that death is the price we must pay for life and that it is now, today, that we must judge everything regarding ourselves and God."

As long as there are people who can ask themselves what they are and who continue to regard life as the supreme value, then suicide will not be made respectable and the vast majority of men will choose life and not death. Symptoms of hope can be seen in the reaction of public opinion whenever someone tries to justify, even for reasons of humanity, what most people in their hearts regard as a weakness, a temporary insanity in a moment of despair.

This was the popular reaction in Sweden to the proposal of Dr. Ingmar Hedenius, Professor of Philosophy at the University of Uppsala, that the Swedish government should set up "suicide clinics," in which those who wanted to put an end to their lives could do so "simply and cleanly." In these clinics, according to Dr. Hedenius, everything possible would be done to persuade would-be suicides to choose life and not death. But if, despite this persuasion, a person still wanted to end his life, he would be helped to do so in a "human" way and not be driven to shooting himself or jumping out a window or using any other such "uncivilized" means.

However, to build clinics of this type would be to acknowledge that man has a right to take his own life. It would give the green light to suicide, which would then be viewed, not as an act of insanity, despair or protest, but as just one among many free choices in the living of one's own life within society.

The problem is a serious one, not least because society today has an obviously ambivalent attitude towards the ethics of suicide, either condemning it outright as insanity and the gravest possible sin or else accepting it as a "normal" act which can be fully justified and is no cause for scandal.

But this acceptance and justification of self-destruction

could be the most subtle and cynical way of denying the serious responsibility that weighs on every one of us whenever anyone, but especially a young person, takes his or her own life because of fear, despair, ennui or illness.

Nowadays many questions are being asked about suicide. Is suicide the greatest act of freedom? (Animals do not commit suicide.) Or is it the ultimate act of slavery? Is it the bravest possible protest in favor of a better life? Or is it, instead, the complete negation of hope?

There is no doubt that there is a growing tolerance of self-destruction, especially if the victim is young and committed to some cause, however unworthy. This tolerance would be good if it were the product of a keener awareness that the world has changed, that our society often takes from us our taste for living, and that now many people too easily reach the limits of despair, wretchedness, loneliness, neurosis or alienation.

Most of us are sometimes driven to say in despair: "No one should be asked to live like this. This is not living but mere existence!" Consequently, we are in some way conscious of all the abuses and repressions and indignities that others may be obliged to bear and that may diminish to some degree their natural repugnance to suicide.

But the fact that we are becoming more used to this serious attack on life is dangerous, especially since the problem of suicide is becoming more acute and since the suicide rate among young people and even among mere children is increasing steadily. Last year in Italy, which is certainly not one of the suicide-prone nations, more than 1,300 young people took their own lives, while 10,000 others tried to do so.

In the past, suicide among older people forced us to think seriously about the redundancy of the elderly in an industrialized society; and today we are being compelled to face up to the isolation of the young in a "young" society.

The problem is made even worse by the change in the "motivation" for suicide. Now many young people kill themselves, not for emotional reasons, but as a protest against somebody or something. Jan Palak was not the only one who killed himself in the streets of Prague; and we hear tell everywhere of young people taking their own lives because, as a French student wrote before setting himself on fire, "It's better to commit suicide than to submit to the dictatorship of society!"

Whatever we may think about the morality of such a gesture, it's hard not to regard it as a despairing appeal to us to become aware of the universe in which we live. Today every suicide has a special importance because it is not just a private, personal matter but an accusation directed against the whole community.

Moreover, the type of person who commits suicide has changed. Formerly, suicide seemed to appeal only to the very wretched or the very famous. But nowadays it has become a mass phenomenon, a social illness, a consumer commodity.

Until quite recently, we used to hear only about the suicides of outstanding figures in history, literature, science or the arts, such as Socrates, Seneca, Nero, Judas, Cleopatra, Hitler, Hemingway, Marilyn Monroe, or Yasunari Kawabata. But now when we switch on the news or open a newspaper we are confronted with an ever-increasing number of suicides among "ordinary" people—students, servant girls, workers, teachers.

Now it is neurosis that drives people to suicide; and neurosis is liable to strike almost anyone. A well-known journalist once remarked to me, "Actually, we are all candidates for suicide these days. All we need is just one more straw to break our backs."

Certainly, many more people commit suicide than we hear about or than the official figures show. For example, it is quite likely that we never get the true suicide figures for the sons and daughters of influential people who have the means of hiding the identity of a suicide or who can afford to take their children who have attempted suicide to private clinics where they are not registered officially as such. There are probably more suicides in prisons than we hear about, and many people undoubtedly succeed in persuading their doctors to put an end to their hopeless suffering. Finally, quite a few "accidents," especially automobile accidents, are really camouflaged suicides.

This "liberalization" of suicide poses problems for religion and the churches, especially when we realize that it is not just the mentally ill who kill themselves but normal, healthy young people who have given no previous signs of being unbalanced. A psychiatrist remarked to me, "Even if we examined closely the history of every suicide and found some psychical abnormality in each case, we would see that it would often be no greater than that which we could discover in any one of us who continue to live without the least thought of doing away with ourselves."

Hence the real reasons for suicide will always be difficult to unravel. As one writer puts it, "Our first impression of a suicide is his absolute negativity. But this is only a superficial judgment since we are very far from knowing his inner life. Each one of us is unique, and so is every suicide. . . . Suicide is always committed in the first person singular since both life and death are always performed in the first person."

We cannot speak about suicide without speaking about life. Hence suicide poses a grave problem for religion as well as for anthropology. This is so even though every suicide is equally mysterious. The writer just quoted goes on to say, "The suicide cannot be held culpable, nor is he necessarily insane, nor should he be regarded as a martyr." But others, both sociologists and moral theologians, believe that we must make a distinction between two main types of suicide based on their motives for taking their own life. Thus some kill themselves because they positively desire death. These are the "philosophical" suicides, one of whom was the only Japanese writer to win the Nobel Prize for Literature, Yasunari Kawabata, who committed suicide at the age of seventy-two because he believed that "death is the quintessence of beauty."

Then there are those who commit suicide as a gesture to help others love life more, such as those who kill themselves as a form of protest, or who undertake fasting to death for religious motives, or the martyrs who give up their lives in defense of their faith.

How do these two types of suicide stand in the eyes of God and of the churches? How are they regarded by

Christianity, which preaches life and hope and belief in
the resurrection?

A modern theologian and philosopher writes: " The
truly Christian man never despairs even in situations as
desperate as those of today because he knows that his
Lord has already won the victory and that his task is to
carry on that victory. But the suicide refuses to believe
in and work for that end because he thinks that the liberation of mankind is impossible or because he has been
frustrated in trying to achieve it. Christ *died;* He did
not commit suicide. His death was, in practical terms,
a total defeat since the Gospel message was not accepted
by the people to whom it was first delivered. The Christian faith consists precisely in being ready to die, but not
to kill oneself, for the sake of a liberation, the seeds of
which we sow in tears and which others will reap rejoic-
ing."

Yet this same theologian goes on to say that we should
have great respect for those young people who choose suicide because of a "feeling of frustration at finding that all
their efforts at changing existing structures have been
futile." And therefore, he asserts, "This ... is not a con-
sciously evil act, and hence the Church must be very careful because we are here faced with a pathological condition, an interior imbalance between the principle of pleasure and the principle of destruction. But this pathological condition is a product of the society in which we live.
Therefore we cannot become accusers, because it is we
who are, in reality, responsible for the suicidal gesture."

From the time of St. Augustine, the Church's attitude
toward suicides has been very severe, denying them Christian burial. But biblical studies have placed the Church
in an embarrassing position as regards the condemnation
of certain forms of suicide. Although the Mosaic Law did
proclaim, "Thou shalt not kill," it did not contain any ex-
plicit condemnation of such people as Samson, Saul or
Abimelech, all of whom caused their own deaths. And it
did not even condemn Judas.

Tertullian praised the young maiden Pelagia, who chose
death rather than surrender her virginity and who was
recognized as a saint. And St. Jerome eulogized a young

man of twenty who starved himself to death doing penance.

And what of our Lord? Actually, the Gospel does not contain any direct condemnation of suicide. Judas was censured for betraying Christ but was not reproached specifically for committing suicide. Some even hold that Christ allowed Himself to be killed since He did not ask or permit the Apostles to defend Him. And He also said, "Greater love has no man than this, that a man lay down his life for his friends" (Jn 15:13).

Furthermore, there are some who ask themselves if the Christian God, who is not a jealous God but a fount of freedom, really wishes to deny man the freedom to be, in conscience, the master of his own death. Was it not God Himself who brought to man the awareness of his total, radical freedom? Drieu de Rochelle, the French writer whose third attempt at suicide was successful, observed that faith in the immortality of the soul can be used as an argument for suicide because the Christian knows that he can be united with his God both in life and in death.

Before shooting himself, a young sociology student wrote, "God, you who are the Truth, help me to believe in you, to see you. I love you, and I want to die. . . ." Elsewhere he had written, "Mine was an infinite, inexorable, unyielding loneliness." The editor of this student's diary wrote, "His suicide was a futile gesture whereby he wished to kill death, not life. And this very gesture may have been his greatest act of love."

The suicides of such earnest young people are usually the result of their sincere, yet despairing, efforts to find a meaning for their existence. As the sociology sudent's mother remarked, his suicide happened because "we were unable to appreciate his inner struggle."

Shortly after attempting to kill himself, another young man confessed, "I'm nineteen. A few months ago I wanted to commit suicide by jumping out a window because I was tired of struggling in this repressive society which allows no one to create anything original. I had fought in every way I could, first as a Christian and then as a Marxist. But I could find no breathing space anywhere.

... Everyone tries to buy you or impose their own ideas on you. And so I told myself one day that the best thing to do would be to end it all. I couldn't accomplish anything important in life, so I thought that perhaps I'd be able to do so in death."

The mother of the young sociology student, of whom we spoke above, later said to me, "Shortly before he died, my son wrote, 'Seeing how absurd death is, I wonder if there may not be something worth living for?' What were the reasons that drove him to do what he did? He loved life; he was always looking for the truth; he believed in his fellowman; and he worked hard for many good causes. But nobody can know for sure the reason for his decision. What happens between a man and his God at such a tragic moment will always be a secret. . . . My son's death has helped me to understand all those other young people who choose the same sad end, though they may do so for quite different reasons. I realize now that the suicides of those youngsters are not just the concern of the psychiatrists, the sociologists or the families involved, but that they are important to every one of us since we all have helped to undermine faith in such things as the family, peace, freedom, brotherhood, love, church, as well as faith in God."

While suicide may be a gesture of protest, it can also be a substitute for a life that cannot be lived fully and freely. Where it is not possible to exercise with dignity one's freedom of conscience and creativity, neither hope nor the joy of living can flourish.

Many people complain that we are doing little or nothing to help the thousands of young men and women who every day are trying to kill themselves; that there are no special clinics, with a sufficiently human atmosphere, for assisting these desperate young people, no centers to which they can go to recuperate psychologically, no one trained to understand them. That is quite true; there are few, if any, such services available. But even if we had them, they would not be sufficient, because they would not get at the root cause of suicide among the youth of the world. And that root cause lies very deep. It is in society itself, where the young people live, study, work, suffer and love.

We must either acknowledge that these young people are different from us, that they have discovered values which we have forgotten or never even knew about, or else we must give up any serious attempt at helping them.

It's not a question of closing our eyes to their obvious faults or of being heavily paternalistic. Instead, we must be just and honest with a generation that has a right to express itself in its own original way. We can see how true this is when we realize that we ourselves still complain occasionally that we were not allowed to live our own lives freely when we were young.

Professor Luccarelli, Head of Psychiatry at the Ospedale Maggiore in Milan, Italy, and the foremost Italian expert on suicide, has studied all the recent attempted suicides in the Milan province, and he concludes, "I must first state that the vast majority of these young people are sane. They are inquisitive and want to feel free; free of a culture and a technology that makes life for them monotonous, rigid and suffocating. The moment arrives when a young person realizes that if he is not to put himself outside the ordinary laws and rules of society, he must follow the well-trodden paths marked out by those who preceded him. It is at this point that he rebels; and, to my mind, he is right in doing so, because I am convinced that if we are to have a new world and new ideas, they must come from the young people."

Professor Luccarelli goes on to say that we must do our best to see that this rebellion by youth is not used by others for their own selfish ends, "since this would be the worst confidence trick that could be played on any young person, an unpardonable swindle. If a young man or woman sees that this is happening, then the drama— and very often the suicide—occurs."

According to the Professor, we often don't understand that today many young people and even children are much more mature than we suspect. As a famous psychologist once said in another context, "I have just been speaking to a *child* of forty years of age and a *woman* of twelve. The mother is the forty-year-old child, and her daughter is the twelve-year-old woman."

23

A Letter to the "Hard-Liners"

I often get letters from "hard-liners" and, naturally, they say harsh things about me. But most of my correspondents are from the great mass of those who are the victims of intransigence, of the "hard lines" taken by others.

Now, having to bear with intransigence is like having your freedom threatened or even curtailed. But I don't know what to say to those who have to suffer from the intransigence of others, because I'm convinced that you cannot combat another's "hard line" by taking a "hard line" yourself. At the same time, however, I feel that attacking anyone's freedom is a crime against the Creator who made each of us free.

Today we are living at a paradoxical moment in history. Although there is great awareness of human dignity, there is also a growing apprehension about the consequences of this wider acknowledgement of man's freedom. The "hard-liners" know that recognition of each man's supreme dignity endangers all privileges and entrenched interests. Therefore, they resist fiercely the spread of tolerance, and

135

they use people's fear of disorder and the remnants of their ancestral serf mentality to bolster up the rule of force.

The weed of intransigence grows in every field; it takes root in the nooks and crannies of every type of institution, both old and new. We find it among those who love each other as well as among those who hate each other, among those who pray as well as among those who blaspheme. Nor is intransigence the monopoly of the intellectuals.

It is the inability to see that the least of men has a lot to teach others; that no one has a corner on truth; that the man who listens is wiser than the one who declaims; that it's more intelligent to search than to adopt a defensive attitude; that the man who asks for things is richer than the one who takes them by force; that he who proposes his views is more a man than the one who imposes them.

The "hard-liner" basically denies the dignity of man because he believes that he is better than everyone else. He doesn't even try to learn because he thinks he knows it all. And he is a grave trial of patience to simple folk, who are the most defenseless against being enslaved.

The opposite of intransigence is not weakness but respect for the beliefs of others.

It is not intransigence on my part if I defend, with conviction, enthusiasm and emotion, my own discovery, my own little nugget of truth. That is simply a necessity for anyone who believes in life.

It is not intransigence to cry out to one's fellowmen, "I have seen the mark of God's footsteps across the face of the earth!"—provided that one is also prepared to stop and listen, courteously and with interest, when another man proclaims with equal conviction, "I feel that the world is empty of any trace of God!"

It is not intransigence to announce one's atheism if one is ready to listen attentively to another's reasons for his belief in God.

Intransigence is a lack of confidence in the possibility that one's neighbor will be saved. It is being in a hurry to condemn; it is a yearning for power, a taste for victory. The opposite of intransigence is faith in man. It is the rejection of despair, the calm, though sad, acceptance of my brother's refusal to take the best gift I can offer him.

It is the absence of every hint of condemnation, the unquenchable belief that it is never too late for anyone to be saved.

It is the patience and tenderness of Jesus of Nazareth, who would not break a bruised reed or quench a smoking wick (see Mt 12:20).

It is feeling the deep yet serene sorrow of seeing the rich young man in the Gospel deliberately turning down Christ's invitation to perfection, while not allowing oneself the luxury of condemning him.

It is the infinite patience of the sun, which continues to shine warmly even on the sheaves that have already been reaped and bound.

It is the greatness of being able to go on believing that stones can still be turned into soft bread, not by a miracle, but because we want them to.

It is the conviction that it is better to love someone than convince him; better to believe in him than to convert him; better to accept him than indoctrinate him.

It is hard to love the great ones of the earth. Hence they are either feared or flattered, which is the bitter price they pay for their intransigence.

When Peter, arrogant and intransigent, wanted to stop Christ from carrying out His mission by going to His death, our Lord expressed His repugnance for His apostle's intervention and even called him "Satan." But when Peter, weak and humble, asked Christ, "Lord, to whom shall we go? You have the words of eternal life," our Lord was touched and praised him.

I believe that the "hard-liners" will never be able to awaken in others the irresistible need to make themselves loved and so feel alive.

Intransigence is a frost of the spirit; it kills the flowers of love and understanding before they can bloom.

24

God Never Has Second Thoughts

When I say that God never has second thoughts, I mean that He has no desire to revive the past.

Among the many false ideas that people have of God is the notion that He longs to see the customs and fears of the past restored.

This idea must be corrected no matter how much it may appeal to those who would like to return to the authoritarianism and dictatorship of the past for the sake of religion, for this would be to act like atheists, or rather, like pagans, since atheists are not usually inclined to be authoritarians. It is necessary to state plainly that the Christian God wants no part of those dregs of ancient political systems.

The true God is neither afraid of the future nor desirous of turning back to the past. He is never tempted to rebuild a social order which had little regard for liberty and justice, both of which have been won only at great sacrifice.

However, broadly speaking, people regard the past in two different ways. Some want to turn the clock back in politics, in religion, in everything, while others are afraid that it may be possible to do so. To my mind, the latter are the more truly human ones.

Therefore, to say that God does not have second thoughts is, in a way, to give a definition of God in the present historical context.

But of what God?

Certainly not the God of those faithful heirs of the Israelites who, in their long pilgrimage through the desert towards the Promised Land, yearned to return to the flesh-pots of Egypt because they found the bread of adventure and the water of deferred hope too little to their liking. But freedom lay ahead, across the desert, and not behind them.

The God who does not have second thoughts is the God of the Bible, the God of the prophets, the God of Abraham, the God who continually condemned His people, not only when they were tempted to turn back, but also whenever they felt like stopping, pitching their tents permanently in any place and ceasing to be nomads, that is, explorers in search of new territory. Consequently, He is the God who always pushes on, the God who never stands still, because He has infinity before Him.

He is Jesus of Nazareth, who called Himself by the significant title of "Son of *Man*."

He is the God who rejects only those who give up fighting for man's liberation.

This is the only way one can be a real atheist, since any sincere effort to save or free other men is a Christian gesture, a gesture of belief in God.

Least of all does God have second thoughts about His greatest act of "insanity," the Incarnation, His decision to become man, truly and forever, with all the risks and all the consequences of that decision. This is the most marked act of "insanity" in history, and we still have not succeeded in believing that it really happened. God does not repent of it, but we find it so hard to take in that we go on as if it had never occurred.

The incredible paradox is that often the atheists seem to understand the Incarnation better than we Christians do. They act as if man actually was the most important being on earth, while we don't. We may pay lip service to the Incarnation, but we regard many things as much more important than man.

Whether we like it or not, we Christians know that our God is not a hidden God, nameless and faceless, but that He has a very real face, the face of a man, and a name, the name of every human being.

Thus in order to understand something about God, we must approach Him through the mystery of man; we must look in men's eyes and learn from them what God's name is.

And God is not sorry for having arranged things like this. The day will never come when He will say, "Very well! I'm tired of being a man. I'm going back to heaven, so don't look for me any more among men. You will have to seek me in the solitude and mystery of my Divinity. Then, the farther you are from men, the easier you will see my face." God's actions are final and irreversible. He is unchanging and does not regret anything He has done, because He made His choice in eternal, infinite freedom.

Obviously, we humans can never act as decisively and as finally as God. Our minds are finite, and there are few things in our past which we would not erase or alter. Our view is very limited and we can act only from moment to moment; and although we believe and act on the eternal truths of faith, even the most righteous among us "falls seven times" a day.

We have to regret many of our actions because they were wrong or incomplete. Still, we know that every time anyone has done or uttered something profoundly true, it has remained and no one has been able to erase it. Words and actions of this kind speak for themselves, even though it be from a prison cell.

God Himself has told us that He will not take anything back: "Heaven and earth will pass away, but my words will not pass away" (Mk 13:31).

What does "Heaven will pass away" mean? It means that religions will pass away, that all the well-intentioned but foolish ideas we have about God will be superseded.

And what does "earth will pass away" mean? It means that all our ideologies, cultures, philosophies—in a word, all our idols—will pass away.

Dietrich Bonhoeffer said, "God is faithful, not to our

hopes, but to His promises"—two very different things. Unfortunately, many of our hopes are not truly human because, if fulfilled, they would be harmful to someone and would end by enslaving him in some way.

God never goes back on His promises, which were not made just for a privileged few, the really good people, but for us all since, unlike us, He is not a racist. He does not go back on His word, for "He is not the God of the dead, but of the living" (Mt 22:32). And He once said, "Let the dead bury their dead"—harsh words, indeed, and ones which make us tremble every time we read them.

Our God does not favor those who do not believe in life, those who are too ready to say, "That's quite enough!" Rather is He the God of those who know that it's preferable to die living than to live dying, that the only true life is built up with effort, piece by piece, and that for him who has faith, joy is not dead on earth.

Especially God does not repent of that great gift of freedom which He has given to man and which makes man like Him. Many people would have God announce one morning that He regretted having given us free will and that He is going to suspend it, for a while at least. Then at last we would have order, honesty, purity, charity and obedience! But God is not sorry for having made us free, and it is up to us to achieve peace, brotherly love and innocence by giving up our hatred, wars and impurity.

This gift of freedom is so great that to take it from someone or prevent him from exercising it is the gravest offense against God, the worst blasphemy, the most brutal atheism. It is like preventing a man from being God, from sharing God's own life. No man may shackle another's freedom for any reason or at any cost. All he can do is defend it.

That is why, even in the Church, whenever men yearn for what has been and are afraid of what may happen, and when this fear and yearning cause them to chain the consciences of others, it is because Christ has been betrayed.

The true church of Christ is present only in that man who has the courage to keep pressing onward even though he may be making a mistake, even in the midst of pain and darkness, even though he is advancing into the unknown, risking the tranquility of the faith he has hitherto acquired.

Pessimism has never been Christian.

It's true that the brutal realities of everyday life make it almost impossible to feel we are getting anywhere; we seem to be already in the last days described in the Book of Revelations. The future of man on earth continues to be very uncertain and bitterly ambiguous.

But we must believe and act on the belief that men will triumph even though the victory will cost dearly; that those who have hope have already won because in their hearts there is still an incredible potential of unexpressed love and unrealized creativity.

Mao Tse Tung once said that patience is a characteristic of all true revolutionaries.

Impatience is reactionary.

Hope is always a bet on man and life.

Today we feel inclined to think that everyone and everything has a price tag. But that is not so. There are many upright men who have no price; and while even one such man remains alive, the world will not come to a grinding halt, since he alone is stronger than the rest: he is like a candle in the middle of a forest, able to set the whole world ablaze again.

We can buy the death of an upright man, but not his life.

The death of Christ cost thirty pieces of silver, but no one was able to buy His Resurrection.

God never repents of these realities, these hopes.

People can be divided into atheists and believers, rich and poor, old and young, exploiters and exploited. All these categories do exist, but the most radical difference between men is that which exists between those who accept the world as it is and those who want to make it different, more credible and more in harmony with those profound demands of freedom and creativity that even the most alienated among us feel within them.

As long as some of us are unhappy with things as they are, there is still room for hope.

And we must remember that it's not we who are the most eager to have a different world but the outcasts, the enslaved and the wretched, because they are the ones who possess nothing and hope for everything; it is they upon whom the heaviest burden of slavery has fallen.

They are still the most disposed to accept the coming of the kingdom; they least of all want to revive the past, which, for them, was a long history of tears and oppression; they are the most attentive to the God of the living and not of the dead, the God of the least of men and not of the privileged classes.

They are the ones who are really alive; and they are always ahead of the rest of men even though they come last in the world parade.

25

Without Prophets, Hope Dies

Christ used very harsh words in condemning those of
His people who "killed the prophets," because the prophets
of every era are the ones who keep alive men's last sparks
of hope.

The prophet anticipates the future and hence prepares
the way for progress.

He alerts us every day to our responsibilities and reveals
to us our most secret sins.

He shows us what we should be but don't have the courage even to attempt.

He is the salt that stings but cures. He is the one who
constantly stirs up the waters of our life so that they don't
stagnate.

Hence we regard him with a strange mixture of love
and hate. We all love a prophet; yet, in a way, we'd like
to kill or silence him if we could.

Prophets have always proved to be rather inconvenient
for the systems of the world, including those of today.
And so the fate of the prophet has never been a happy one.
Prophets are, as it were, the last word of our conscience,

145

which we would like to silence precisely because it is right.
The prophet is usually feared because he is the voice of
God Himself, proclaiming, denouncing, revealing, awaken-
ing and showing us that no one is so sinless that he can
afford to throw the first stone at any of his neighbors.

It is the prophet, too, who shows us that today it's not
easy to divide men into the oppressors and the oppressed,
for we all carry the blood of Cain in our veins and need
a continuous conversion because no one can say that he
does not exploit others, great or small.

I once sat beside the wife of a prominent politician while
her husband was delivering a brilliant speech against the
exploitation of others. During the speech, she leaned over
and whispered to me, "Just listen to him! He's an ex-
ploiter himself. He has made me a slave to the house
and the children!"

But while we are all a little afraid of the prophet, the
ones who fear him most are those in power, the tyrants,
the experts, the self-righteous. And so most of the prophets have come to a sticky end. Christ was more than a
prophet, and therefore He had to be killed. Indeed, as St.
Luke tells us, they would have done away with Him even
sooner if it had not been for a miracle. More than once
He lamented the fact that Israel always killed her prophets.

Herod had John the Baptist decapitated; Manasseh had
Isaiah sawn in half; and all the Apostles were subjected
to martyrdom. In modern times, prophets are locked up
in psychiatric hospitals, tortured or shot. Yes, we still
have prophets today. The world cannot do without them,
nor can the Church. Vatican II tells us that every baptized
person has an obligation to be a prophet to the world.

The first Christians were all prophets; and so they were
all martyrs.

Yes, we still have prophets today, even though we don't
like the idea. And we shall go on having them even though
we keep killing them, or mocking them, or isolating them,
which is crueller than taking their lives outright.

Today, however, we do not normally kill our prophets
as our brutal ancestors did. No, we are more refined, and
more cynical, and so we have found a neat way of render-

ing them harmless. Piously we ask ourselves, "Who could possibly tell which prophet is true and which is false? Who can assure us that so-and-so is a real prophet, at least while he's still alive? And didn't Christ Himself tell us to be on our guard against false prophets? The best way to protect ourselves from being deceived is to refuse to listen to any of them. Let Canon Law take its slow but sure course, and when both we and they are dead, the Church will decide and will make amends to them if they really were prophets."

This is certainly the safest way to deal with any potential prophets; and it also ensures that they won't bother us. But let's be honest. Our fear of prophets has made us more diligent in unmasking the false ones than in discovering the true. As usual, when we proclaim loudly that we are thirsting for the truth, we are really only trembling with fear lest it should be found. Hence, the word of God, which is always prophetic, is uncomfortable for us.

Hence, too, for a long time the Church practically forbade the ordinary faithful to read the Bible. At most, she permitted some sections of it to be read in Latin in church. But when the prophetic words of the Bible are translated into our vernacular, applied to our lives and put into practice by the new prophets, they are very unsettling, not least for some vested interests, clerical and lay.

One thing is clear: when we try to discredit as false prophets those who are endangering our comfortable system, we are really only making sure that there will be no true prophets. We have made up our own special rules to apply to any outbreak of prophecy, and it is curious how we normally conclude that a prophecy is false for the very reasons which prove that it is true. We should ask ourselves a question that may be dangerous: "Instead of having such an irrational fear of false prophets, why don't we instead fear the lack of true prophecy, both inside and outside the Church?"

Every act of the Church, whether of its teaching authority or of its pastoral mission, must have a certain element of prophecy if we are to feel that it is genuine. Where that element is lacking, we should ask ourselves seriously whether or not we are being confronted with the "non-Church," the "non-Christ," the "non-word of life." For once, let's stop looking for signs of false prophecy and have the courage to search instead for the signs of true prophecy so that it won't escape us without our even being aware that it has come and gone.

According to the best biblical tradition, the indisputable signs of true prophecy are:

1. Every prophetical word and act must be a jolt to the wishful thinkers, the sleepyheads, the bureaucrats, the diplomats and the bosses of every kind.

2. Prophecy does not compromise. It is either "Yes!" or "No!", never "Yes, but..." It has the certainty of a mission received from God. The prophet's obstinacy is not a sin but a guarantee.

3. The more humble, simple and interior the origin of a prophecy, the truer it is.

The crowds said of Christ, "Where did this man get this wisdom and these mighty works? Is not this the carpenter's son?" (Mt 13:54-55). Neither doctorates in theology, nor high ecclesiastical rank, nor religious "blue blood" guarantees that the prophet will be accepted and his message believed.

The prophet will never be accepted fully. Moreover, his mission will usually be called into question by those who can do so and who have no wish to be converted.

Prophecy is never confined within the boundaries of its country or religion of origin. It knows no frontiers; it speaks to everyone and, where necessary, through the mouth of the outcast or the stranger—the Canaanite woman or the Samaritan, Balaam's donkey or the non-Christian, the atheist or the poorest street sweeper.

Generally, the prophet's words will be rejected by those around him and will not be understood by those whose job it is to preach the truth. He will be understood better by the ordinary people than by the learned, better by the least of all than by the "Pharisees." Pope John, for example, was received more warmly by some unbelievers than by many "devout" Catholics, by simple folk than by certain Cardinals.

The language of prophecy is always clear, although it

can be full of symbolism. It is always harsh, yet encouraging, for those who listen to it, as happens in any encounter with the living God.

The prophet knows that he is alone, that he is a continuous sign of contradiction and that he will be rejected by those who are well-situated in life. Yet he still retains a deep joy in his heart and a great inner security because he is the bearer of a truth which he himself may not succeed in understanding fully, a message which is greater than man even though it is meant for him. But that message is destined for real men; and seldom are we that.

If we are honest with ourselves, we must confess that a large part of what we easily accept as the word of God, the teachings of the Faith and the doctrine of the Church, is merely the voice of "false prophets" who do not possess the guarantees of true prophecy, that is, scandal, contradiction from those in power, a self-assurance that does not shrink from inquiry, the call to true conversion and to make "each day new," and the invitation to sacrifice one's life if necessary.

Words, deeds and teachings that spare us all these dangers and leave us undisturbed will scarcely commend themselves to us as possessing the hallmark of the true prophecy of Christ, which was a "scandal and contradiction" to so many who heard it.

26

A Letter to the "New" Men

Most people live only to keep or increase what they have and are continually afraid that they will lose it. They are full of fear; they are "old," as opposed to "new," men. To justify their attitude, they say that everything new is dangerous and that everything pertaining to the past is safe. These are not the "new" men to whom I wish to write this letter.

I know that there are few truly "new" men around, but I have hopes that the desire to be "new" will begin to stir in the hearts of many. Actually, the "new" is merely the "more" for which everyone is hoping and seeking, and about which they are dreaming even when the fear of losing what they already possess prevents them from launching out to search and create.

Paradoxically, both fear of the new and desire for something more exist side by side within man, like two distinct personalities. But fear is older than man himself, and it often prevails over the desire for adventure and improvement.

The way we regard the feast of Christmas is symptomatic of this. We seem to make Christmas the center of our security, to conecntrate in it all our longing for protection and a mother's love. And so we have turned it into a rite of family reunion, a time for special emphasis on encounter, pardon and peace.

Christmas can be, and happily is, a poetic interlude in a prosaic year, necessary both for families, which are becoming more dispersed, and for the individual, who is becoming more alienated from himself and from his neighbors. It is, however, the greatest feast of the "new" since it is the feast of Christ's *birth*. Yet in our celebration of it, we are almost totally preoccupied with our longings for the past and think little about reaching out for the future.

It is the starting point for humanity's march toward a world that is different and unknown, one which has never existed before and in which, in the words of the prophet Isaiah, "They shall beat their swords into plowshares.... The wolf shall dwell with the lamb" (Is 2:4; 11:6). It is the point at which God gave history a new direction through the birth of the new Man who is as truly man and as truly new as He is truly God.

We shall never succeed in being true men if we do not lose our fear of being born anew, of leaving, if necessary, our homes and country to go we know not where.

Hence our victory, our definitive discovery, the last dimension, the unforeseeable, is in front of us, in something which we still do not know and have not seen.

Although that which already exists may be good, it is already old; it is "possible" and hence lacks the irresistible charm of the impossible, which is still untouched, unsullied and untried.

I have never been able to understand how people can seriously call themselves revolutionaries when they are so afraid of the new that they are quite happy to take things as they are, provided that they can call them by new names, or paint them a new color, or use them to grab power for themselves.

The "new" men are those who are sure that there is no such word as "Enough!" They are the ones who look to the future, not as a continuous process of growth, but as containing the possibility of new discoveries and the thrill of unforeseen turns in history.

God's becoming man was not the culmination of a steady evolutionary process but a leap forward to something entirely new. It was an absolutely gratuitous and utterly disconcerting act of "insanity," the explosion of the new into the realm of the old.

The "new" men are those who achieve here and now what the prophets foretold as the realities of tomorrow; for the new is simply the actualization of the future.

Christ was not just a prophet; He began to live life in a new way, looked at history with new eyes and did things which no one had ever done before. He was not content merely to preach the resurrection of the dead but Himself rose for the dead.

He did not confine Himself to cleansing the Temple, to making concordats or setting up unions but preached and brought it about that men do not need to adore in a temple but to worship in spirit and truth; He taught that man is more important than the Sabbath; and He founded a new, absurd kingdom in which one wins by losing, is born by dying, and commands by obeying.

In order to achieve the new, He did not hesitate to condemn the old, not as bad, but as outworn, as not-new and hence as noncreative. He created the new, not in solitude, but among men, in the dust, bustle and strife of the marketplace. Only thus can the past be redeemed with dignity and without repudiating or belittling it. The fire of a new history can and must be kindled from the still-glowing ashes of what men have been.

The "new" man is one who suffers from fear, not of losing what he has, but of being unable to possess that which he does not yet own but which he feels belongs to him and is indispensable for his total fulfillment.

27

Hope Is Not Useless

If I had to say what people have most often asked me to give them, I wouldn't have to think twice about my answer: *hope*.

No, hope is not useless, nor is it impossible if one really wants it, searches and asks for it.

It is so necessary if we are to go on living that we die if we are incapable of pronouncing its name.

Yet hope is the most difficult thing in life.

Only the immature can say that it is easy and that it is given to us at a discount.

Everyone needs hope—saints and sinners, learned and ignorant.

Despair, the absence of all hope, is hell.

Yet to hope means to believe that hope is stronger than despair.

True hope is never placed in a thing but in "someone."

The man who has lost hope in everyone ceases to be a man.

It is despair, the lack of hope, and not evil that utterly destroys us.

155

Evil can wound us, crucify us, plunge us into darkness, and even kill us. But all that means nothing if hope is still alive in our hearts. As our Lord said, "Do not fear those who kill the body but cannot kill the soul" (Mt 10: 28).

Hope is a scandal and madness if we do not believe that there is something within us greater than ourselves.

Indeed, everything around us seems to prove that hope is a delusion.

But precisely for this reason, hope is neither madness nor childish optimism.

It does not consist in ignorance of the elements of despair that are so much in evidence all around us. When the hopeful man hears that one brother has killed another, a father has raped his daughter, a friend has betrayed his friend and that someone has sold his soul for a little power, while society looks drowsily on, drugged by easy living, he does not just say, "These things have always been done and aren't really all that important. Anyway, what can I do about them? I've got to make a living!"

Nor does he say, more piously, "It's all a mystery which God will explain in the next life."

No, hope calls a spade a spade and does not hesitate to apply the terms "murderer," "thief," and "hypocrite" to those who deserve them. Yet it goes on believing, perhaps without understanding why, that man is more than his actions and that hope will have the last word.

When Galileo was imprisoned by the Holy Office, he is said to have murmured, "But it still moves!" So also, although man is burdened with the thought of approaching death and the scandal of humanity becoming less and less human, he still goes on saying, "But man will continue to choose life!"

Hope conquers by dying or, rather, by allowing itself to be killed.

Life is born from death, but hope places the accent on life rather than on death: and this is the difference between the stoic and the believer.

Accepting death is stoicism, whereas Christianity means proclaiming that Christ has overcome death.

Christ was great, not because He accepted death, but

because He looked beyond it. The saints do not take their own lives; yet they may allow themselves to be killed, believing that death has already been conquered. Peter said to the Jews, "You . . . killed the Author of life" (Acts 3:15), but not, "You killed life."

Hence he who dies without losing hope never hates, because he knows that there is neither place nor taste for hatred in the realm of life. Victory always belongs to him who forgives, because forgiveness is the seed of resurrection.

It is good to remove evil, but it is a difficult and dangerous task. Therefore Christ counselled leaving the weeds in the wheat field until the harvest.

To forgive does not mean accepting attacks on innocence, life or love.

I forgive the evil done to me, but not that which is done to my neighbor.

I allow myself to be killed, but I do not allow others to kill my fellowman.

Although Christ later permitted Himself to be killed, He did not let the Jews kill the adulterous woman.

Even though hope often conquers by dying, it is bound up with life, with that which is born. Therefore God is always and only where something is being born. At Christ's death, the tombs were emptied.

But things are born in us only when we allow them to be, and this is the only truly active passivity.

All those who believe in hope accept defeat by death without falling into despair.

Hope is believing that only those actions which we do without hope are useless.

The pessimist is one who cannot believe that the stones can speak and that the Church can be born again only by dying.

The optimist is one who believes that the stones can speak by themselves and that the oppressor will be overthrown without bloodshed.

But the realist, on the contrary, is the man of hope who will undertake any labor in order to speed up the birth of the new and who will proclaim everywhere, whether in freedom or in chains, that mankind will be victorious.

No wretchedness, no difficulty and no limitations can make us lose the hope of entering into the kingdom of joy, because we know that God became man, like us in all things except sin, but without ceasing to be God.

The victory no longer belongs to the strong, the perfect, the rich, the stoics, for they have been cast down by the weakness of the Christian God, who brought to the world the greatest paradox, that of conquering death by dying.

Stephen, the first Christian martyr, was stoned to death for speaking "blasphemous words against Moses and God" (Acts 6:11), for the price of hope is misunderstanding, isolation, exile, persecution and martyrdom.

To hope is to believe in the impossible and to live as if it were already a reality, because it is real from the moment we believe it is—and it is we who make it possible.

Hope such as this cannot be tolerated by the powerful and the tyrants of the world because it is the wellspring of freedom.

And so the men of hope, the really free men, are sent to their death or locked up in mental hospitals.

Free men do not allow human institutions to become stagnant, and they overthrow idols and superstitions.

Thus while Stephen was shedding his blood in defense of an impossible and intolerable hope, Saul of Tarsus, still unconverted and still exulting in his power to persecute Christians, was a willing witness.